All the Best,
Marilyn Bussey

Trekking Through Northern Labrador
A Woman's Odyssey
Marilyn Bursey

Oceanside Publishing, St. John's, Newfoundland

Published by:
Oceanside Publishing
St. John's, Newfoundland
CANADA

Printed and bound in Canada by Friesen Printers.

ISBN 1-55056-589-3

Cover: *The Torngat Mountains, north of Komaktorvik Lakes.*

Trekking Through Northern Labrador
A Woman's Odyssey

Marilyn Bursey

For Brian, my husband, my friend,
my inspiration.

CONTENTS

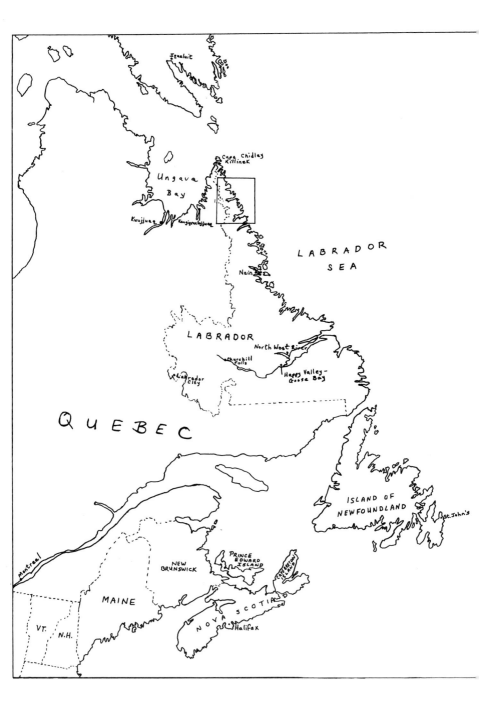

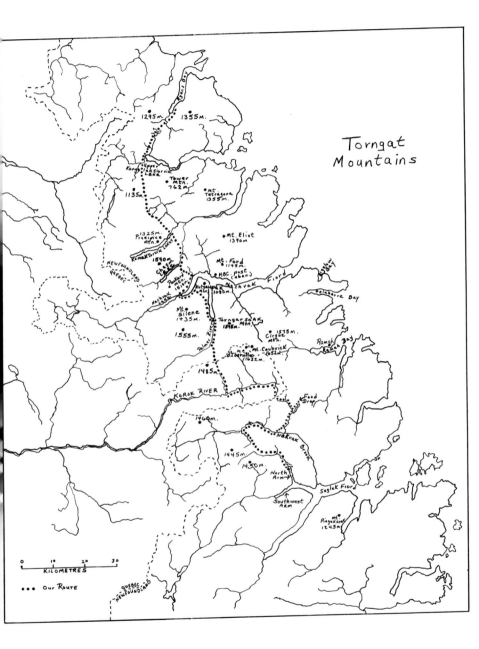

Torngat
Mountains

1295m.   1355m.

Komaktorvik
Lake

Tower
Mtn.
762m.

1135m.

Mt. Tetragona
1355m.

P.1325m.
Precipice
Mtn.

Mt. Eliot
1390m.

Komaktorvik Lake

1540m.

Mt. Ford
1145m.

NEWFOUNDLAND
QUEBEC

HBC Post
(aban.)

Palmer
1515m.

Nachvak Fiord

Nachvak

Kutyaupak
Mtn.
1050m.

Mt.
Silene
1435m.

Torngarsoak
Mtn.
1318m.

1575m.
Cirque
Mtn.

Delabarre Bay

Ramah
Bay

1555m.

Palmer R.

Mt.
d'Iberville
1622m.

Mt. Caubvick
1652m.

1485m.

KOROK RIVER

Food
Drop

1160m.

Nakvak Brook

1445m.

Saglek Fiord

1450m.

North
Arm

Southwest
Arm

Mt.
Pingaksuak
1245m.

0   10   20   30
KILOMETRES

••• Our Route

QUEBEC
NEWFOUNDLAND

CHAPTER 1

THE LURE OF THE NORTH

The Torngats! I had heard my husband, Brian, speak of these magnificent mountains many times. Brian had visited northern Labrador's Torngat Mountains twice before, both times leaving from Nain, the most northerly settlement on the Labrador coast. During his first visit, in 1985, he had travelled as far as Saglek Fiord, an eight hundred kilometre round trip, in a four metre Zodiac inflatable! His second trip, in 1989, had taken him to Nachvak Fiord, even further north, this time in a six metre open fibreglass boat. Each time, Brian made the journey alone. I accompanied him as far as Nain on the second trip, and this was my first taste of Labrador.

Although I had considered continuing north with him in 1989, I felt I was not yet ready for such an adventure. Until that time, my experience with the outdoors had consisted of hikes on developed trails, and camping in parks with washroom and shower facilities.

I recall that my sister and I had camped in a national park many years ago and, during a trip to the lavatory, heard some people mention that there had been a black bear in the area the previous week. After settling into our tent for the night, I lasted about ten minutes. I heard a garbage can rattle in the distance (probably someone dumping their leftovers), but I wasn't taking any chances. We both grabbed our sleeping bags and ran for the car. Even in the car, I couldn't sleep, as I had visions of a big black bear peering through the windows in search of food. To me, camping in the wilderness meant being surrounded by wild animals, especially bears, and things that go "bump in the night". I really wasn't very brave back then - not that I'm all that courageous now, but I have spent much more time in the wilderness and fear of the unknown is not as predominant.

Brian has published several photography books on Newfoundland and Labrador, and his love of hiking, canoeing and camping can be very contagious. I had seen quite a bit of Newfoundland on our outdoor adventures, and his fascination with Labrador was gradually luring me there as well. However, I, like so many others, was not familiar with Labrador. To me, it conjured up images of snow and cold weather for most of the year, with fly infested summers.

THE LURE OF THE NORTH

I spent one night in the tent on that 1989 trip, before Brian departed on his journey north to explore and take photos. We camped on a small island near Nain. The gentle lapping of the waves against the shoreline was soothing and relaxing for Brian, but not for me. I could imagine a polar bear splashing out of the water and coming up to our tent for his next meal - us! It was only during the days that I could really enjoy the tranquility of such a remote place. I needed more experience with wilderness camping before I could take on anything like our Torngat adventure.

One thing that our 1989 trip accomplished was that Labrador was now in my blood. I loved it! My previous thoughts on Labrador changed completely with my first visit. We spent some time in Happy Valley-Goose Bay, before heading north to Nain, and Brian took me to visit the air base at Goose Bay, as well as the beautiful and historic town of North West River. He also took me on the dirt road that leads from Happy Valley to the community of Churchill Falls. Although we didn't have time to drive all the way to Churchill Falls, we did go as far as Muskrat Falls, and to Gull Island Rapids further west. There was a soft carpet of caribou moss underfoot as we walked through the woods. The falls and rapids were beautiful, and it was sad to think that all this might eventually be dammed to allow for hydro-electric development. Brian and I decided that we would return to canoe this river before it disappeared beneath a couple of large man-made reservoirs. Up to that time, I had only canoed one short river in Newfoundland, but I thought it might be interesting to canoe this one.

During that first trip, I realized just what lured people to Labrador. As we were flying in, I asked Brian what all the white was, thinking it was snow. I was told it was sand and caribou moss. Beautiful sand everywhere and lovely warm weather were not what I had expected.

A couple of short canoeing trips early the following year taught me the basics of paddling on a river with some white water, about portaging and lining, and how to spot and avoid rocks ahead of the canoe (most of the time!). All this helped me when we returned to Labrador later that summer to canoe the mighty Churchill. We also visited the actual site of Churchill Falls, near the modern community of the same name. Once one of the largest waterfalls in North America, it is now little more than a trickle, the main flow having been diverted through a huge underground powerhouse in the late 1960s.

The three hundred kilometre canoe trip from Churchill Falls to Goose Bay took eight days, and started my orientation towards wilderness camping and experiencing the remoteness of Labrador. It was a beautiful river to canoe, with breathtaking scenery and an abundance of wildlife. From that time on there was no turning back, and we decided we would hike the Torngats together in July, 1994.

CHAPTER 2

WE ARRIVE IN KUUJJUAQ

Getting to the Torngats is, however, far from easy. While they straddle the Quebec-Labrador border, the Torngats are fifteen hundred kilometres north of our home in St. John's, Newfoundland. More significantly, the nearest inhabited community in Newfoundland and Labrador is Nain, some five hundred kilometres south of where we hoped to begin our journey.

While it might have been possible to arrange boat transportation from Nain, our limited vacation time made such an approach impractical. Moreover, the closest floatplane operators in Labrador were based in Goose Bay and Labrador City, eight hundred kilometres south of our intended destination. Chartering a floatplane for such a distance would have been prohibitively expensive.

TREKKING THROUGH NORTHERN LABRADOR

We next investigated the possibility of access from Ungava Bay. While the small Inuit community of Kangiqsualujjuaq (formerly George River) lay less than two hundred kilometres from our starting point, there were no aircraft charters available there. We were, however, able to determine that such services were available in Kuujjuaq, a somewhat larger community further to the west.

The next few weeks were frustrating ones, as we tried unsuccessfully to make contact with the air charter service in Kuujjuaq. Finally, after numerous telephone calls and faxes, we succeeded in obtaining quotes for drop-off and pickup in the Torngats. However, subsequent faxes to confirm these arrangements received no response, nor did we receive any reply to our request for information on how we could contact the company upon our arrival. It was, therefore, with a certain amount of trepidation that we left St. John's in the early morning of July 15, flying first to Halifax, then to Montreal and, finally, on to Kuujjuaq. We hoped to make contact with the appropriate people at the air charter service in Kuujjuaq when we arrived later that day.

Air service between Montreal and the eastern Arctic is provided by First Air, which operates a modern jet service which lands in Kuujjuaq before proceeding on to Iqaluit on Baffin Island. Kuujjuaq is more than 1,400 kilometres north of Montreal, and the seemingly endless procession of forest, rivers and lakes was a reminder of how much of Canada remains wild and inaccessible. As we neared Kuujjuaq, the landscape gradually changed as the forest gave way to swampy muskeg, broken here and there by scattered rocky outcroppings and clumps of larch and black spruce.

Upon arrival in Kuujjuaq, we telephoned the air charter people, who told us that the Cessna plane, which was to take us to the Torngats, needed a new propeller (I wondered what happened to the old one!). No one seemed to have any knowledge of when a new propeller might be delivered, but we were advised that the winds were too high to fly that day in any event. Meanwhile, the manager of the air charter service said he would send someone to the airport "shortly" to bring us and our gear to the floatplane base which was located a short distance outside town. No one showed up for hours, and we waited in a small office close to the airport until someone finally made a call to remind the air charter people that we were waiting for them. The flies were ferocious, probably reflecting the boggy terrain, and they were about to lock up the building for the day. We never would have survived outside without fly nets. All this was making me very nervous as to what we were getting ourselves into. Brian, however, was so excited about the whole trip that he didn't much care as long as someone showed up eventually.

Kuujjuaq, or Fort Chimo as it was formerly known, has the prefab look typical of the far north. With a population of about 2,000, it is the largest community in Ungava Bay and the administrative centre for this region of Quebec. Most of the inhabitants are Inuit.

The main mode of transportation seemed to be ATVs and a few battered four-wheel-drive vehicles. ATVs were coming and going the whole time we waited at the airport, dropping off and picking up parcels and people. We would have liked to explore the community a bit, but didn't want to take a chance on missing the air charter people when they came for us. We also had quite a bit of gear and didn't want to leave it unattended.

Someone eventually came to pick us up, and we spent the night in a small building owned by the air charter company. The whole area swarmed with mosquitoes, despite the fairly strong breeze, and, when we retrieved a pot of water from the lake, it was swimming with larvae. After we cooked dinner and Brian drank his protein enriched tea (which he said reminded him of boarding house soup!), we spread our sleeping bags on the floor for the night.

We awoke around 4:00 a.m. to a beautiful, still morning; however, by 7:00 the winds were fairly high with heavy, gray clouds scudding across the sky. We assumed we probably wouldn't get to the Torngats that day but, when the pilots arrived for work and received the weather report, we learned the winds were dropping on the Labrador side. Unfortunately they also advised that the area where we were to land had pack ice in the bays and some of the lakes were still frozen. There was a possibility that we would not be able to land in the lake that Brian had marked as a landing point. We could not deviate too much from our original plan because we only had maps for the areas along our intended route, and our time to get to the pickup point was limited.

We decided to take a chance, as Brian was fairly certain that there would be a lake in the area that was not frozen, especially at sea level. The Cessna was still out of operation, so we set out in a Beaver aircraft just before 9:00 a.m. on July 16.

CHAPTER 3

RYANS BAY

As we set out from Kuujjuaq the low cloud cover continued, and the gray waters of Ungava Bay were partially obscured by banks of fog. Soon, squalls of wet snow and sleet spattered against the windshield as we flew over low barren ridges and bedrock outcroppings. I was surprised to see the extent of the snow cover in the lee of the hills at such low elevations.

After about an hour of flying, we passed over the George River and the village of Kangiqsualujjuaq, and then over a fish camp near the mouth of the Korok River. Gradually the weather began to improve and the terrain became more attractive, with higher hills and well drained valleys dotted with small bands of caribou. The Torngat Mountains loomed in the distance, spectacular from the air, and we were anxious to get a closer look.

Brian had planned our trip in great detail. Several months before our journey he had obtained detailed topographic maps of the area and plotted a course through the mountains that followed, to the extent possible, a series of broad glacial valleys. Our route was also planned in a way which would allow us to ford the rivers in the shallowest places and to cross from one valley to another at the lowest elevation, while avoiding the steepest slopes. We planned to hike for eighteen days, starting at a lake near Ryans Bay, about seventy-five kilometres south of Cape Chidley, and working our way south to North Arm in Saglek Fiord. Our pilot was to pick us up there on August 2.

On our flight in, the plane landed at an inland lake about thirty kilometres north of Saglek Fiord to drop off some supplies. Here we left a large, waterproof bag of food, including a couple of beer and soft drinks for a special treat during the last few days of the trip. Brian is very fond of homemade french fries when we're in the great outdoors, so we also included five pounds of potatoes and a bottle of cooking oil, extra propane, and a few staple items. This food drop was intended more as a convenience than a necessity, and we didn't depend on leaving a large quantity of supplies at a halfway point as we thought we might have trouble with bears and foxes getting into our cache. We anticipated being able to stretch the food we carried with us to cover the last few days if animals did get into our dropped off supplies.

Brian was very enthusiastic about the trip and I looked forward to it with nervous anticipation. It would be quite an undertaking. We were travelling a long distance, on foot, in a very wild, remote environment. We had no form of communication with the outside world, and the nearest settlement was almost two hundred kilometres away. We did, however, have a borrowed Emergency Locator Transmitter, or ELT, which could send out a distress signal in case of emergency. That was a great comfort throughout the whole trip. Our families also had the details of our route in the event we weren't at the pickup point on August 2.

I think some of the air charter people at Kuujjuaq believed we were a bit foolish taking on such an expedition. They thought if the bears didn't get us, we would get lost in the mountains or something equally dreadful. Of course, neither of us fits the mould of the sinewy, athletic type (Brian regularly describes us as a couple of middle-aged fat people), and they also saw what we would be carrying!

By noon we had located the lake Brian had chosen as a starting point. Unfortunately, although fairly large, it was shallow and studded with huge boulders. Brian pointed to the blue and, thankfully, ice-free waters of Ryans Bay in the distance. Within a few minutes we had landed and relayed our gear to shore.

The Torngat Mountains from the air.

TREKKING THROUGH NORTHERN LABRADOR

Although I was a bit apprehensive about what we would be facing over the next eighteen days, I was glad to be on solid ground. One thing I absolutely hate is flying in small planes. I always get airsick, and when Brian told me this would be a fairly long flight, I wasn't looking forward to it. Although the view of the mountains from the air was spectacular, I could only enjoy it in small doses. When we landed for the food drop, it gave me a few minutes to get some fresh air. After we took off again and flew north through the rows of gray mountains with their still frozen lakes, Brian kept looking back at me to call my attention to the various points of interest. I paid attention most of the time, but, by the time we were about fifteen minutes from Ryans Bay, I just waved at him to not talk to me. He knew why. He just passed me back the barf bag and later patted me on the knee as we went in for a landing. I was so glad when I got out into the fresh air.

After all our gear was out of the plane, we said good-bye to our pilot and watched as the Beaver rose into the azure sky and disappeared over the mountains. We looked at each other saying, "Well, here we are. It's too late to change our minds now!" My first instinct was to look around for any sign of bears, especially polar bears. The latter are fairly common in this part of Labrador, and, while they are usually found on the headlands and offshore islands, I was not looking forward to the possibility of running into one of these monarchs of the north. It was not a comfortable feeling knowing we were completely on our own if we got into trouble. We were alone with the wildlife and ghosts of these mountains. We knew we had quite a challenge ahead of us.

The author, near Ryans Bay.

CHAPTER 4

STARTING OUR TREK

After the plane disappeared, everything was very still except for the sound of water running down the mountainside and trickling beneath the rocks into the bay. It was Saturday, July 16. The day was cool, but not uncomfortable.

Since this part of Labrador lies well above the tree line, it was necessary for us to carry, not only food and camping equipment, but an ample supply of propane for cooking as well. Brian's pack was an uncomfortable thirty-five kilograms and he carried a rifle in one hand (a necessary protection against possibly unfriendly wildlife) and a waterproof army surplus ammunition case, which contained his camera and lenses, in the other. In total he was weighed down by forty-three kilograms, as determined on our scales before we left home. (On trips of this nature, you eat the heaviest food first!) My pack was much lighter at approximately eighteen kilograms. In addition, I carried my camera case and a small backpack containing the ELT, maps and fly repellent.

The heavy packs and rough talus slopes which made up the eastern shoreline of Ryans Bay initially made for tough going, but we eventually worked our way around to the bottom of the bay. Here, a broad valley led gently away to the south. A few minutes later we surprised a brood of black ducks in a small pool lined with large angular blocks of gneiss. While the adults flew away, most of the young disappeared among the rocks. Although hidden from view, we could hear them complaining loudly as they scrabbled beneath the boulders.

Once we reached the valley, the going was much easier, and we stopped to cook a brunch of fried bologna and toast, as we had not taken the time to have breakfast before we left Kuujjuaq. Nearby, a couple of snow buntings, handsome in their black and white summer plumage, flitted from rock to rock. As we sat on some boulders and looked across the bay, surrounded by snowcapped mountains, I wondered how many other women had walked over these barrens or been in this bay. Probably not many, except the native Inuit women who traversed these valleys with their families many years ago. I felt privileged to be one of the few to experience this northern wilderness.

Our first encounter with the icy-cold streams of these northern mountains occurred later that day. We had walked about seven kilometres since landing, and had come to a shallow stream with a fast current. We crossed where the stream separated into two channels. I was not, however, prepared for the temperature of the water! I had expected it to be cold because of the snow on the mountains, but this water was numbing. After a few seconds, all feeling left my feet and legs. Although my first instinct was to rush to the other side, this was not wise, as the rubble at the bottom of the stream was unstable, and falling into the icy water with a pack on, or twisting an ankle, was not on the agenda for our first day. We were glad to get back to dry land.

The stream flowed through a small valley which provided enough shelter for a few stunted arctic willows, not more than half a metre in height. As it was now after 5:00 p.m., we decided to put up the tent next to a huge snowdrift which offered some protection from the winds which can sometimes sweep through these fiords. It was quite cool by this time, as the sun had gone behind the mountains, and there was a low cloud cover. We gathered some dead willow branches and lit a small fire to help dry our legs. That night, to celebrate our arrival in the Torngats, we cooked a substantial meal of steaks and mushrooms, washed down with a couple of cans of beer. We knew it would be some time before we would have another.

The total distance we planned to hike was about one hundred and thirty kilometres in a straight line, but our overall journey would total two hundred and five kilometres, the result of having to follow the river valleys through the mountains. Brian had checked the contour lines on the maps before we started our trip in order to avoid steep climbs and descents, and would evaluate the maps each evening to adjust our route, as necessary.

As we were carrying our food, fuel, dishes, clothes, tent, sleeping bags, camp rests, and emergency kit on our backs, everything was kept to a minimum. We took only the basic necessities in everything - including clothes. We had to cross streams and brooks every day, so it was impossible to keep dry. As the days went by we became less and less particular about dry feet and dry clothes. Many mornings we put our wet socks and wet pants back on! Sometimes the warm sun and wind dried our clothes as we walked and, if we were lucky enough not to have to cross a brook late in the day, we would have dry clothes to start out the next morning - but not dry sneakers. They did not dry completely for the full time we were there, although they are much lighter and do dry more readily than hiking boots. We wore thinsulate winter jackets which were lightweight and dried quickly. Many days the sun was very warm, but we needed our jackets to provide extra padding to protect our shoulders from the weight of the heavy packs.

A major force that contributed to the character of Labrador was ice. Glaciers rounded and smoothed the rock across wide plateaus, and gouged out existing valleys and structural weaknesses in the bedrock to form long, steep-walled, U-shaped valleys. The moving ice also dug deep cirques and hanging valleys ending in sheer cliffs, and left great piles of fragmented rock as lateral and end moraines. Perhaps the most remarkable glacial features of northern Labrador are the magnificent coastal fiords that, in the case of Saglek and Nachvak in particular, extend inland for tens of kilometres. In some cases, similar features were formed well inland from the existing coast, leaving long, narrow finger lakes surrounded by spectacular cliffs.

Strange as it may seem, however, it is now generally believed that this region was not completely glaciated during the last ice age, the Torngats forming an effective barrier to the ice sheet which covered most of continental North America until about 10,000 years ago. As a result, a number of plants survived here that are now rare in North America and whose closest relatives, geographically speaking, may be in southern Greenland or on the highlands of the Gaspé Peninsula.

Sheltered campsites in the Torngats are limited. The winds sweeping through the mountain valleys and fiords can rip a small dome tent to shreds. We could not take a chance on putting up the tent in an exposed location, as it would be our only shelter for eighteen days.

CHAPTER 5

UPPER KANGALAKSIORVIK LAKE

Our second day, July 17, started out cold with light, misty rain and low cloud. A strong wind blew in our faces. It was a miserable morning, but at least it wasn't raining heavily.

The rather gloomy weather was, however, offset by near perfect walking conditions. Our route led south over a series of broad terraces, perfectly level except for a barely perceptible slope. The ground was firm and dry, and seemed to consist of a fine gravel covered in a short, grassy turf. A large plane could have landed here without difficulty.

We saw several flocks of Canada geese and goslings in a series of small ponds shortly after we broke

23

Moss Campion.

camp. Later, a pair of peregrine falcons wheeled overhead. By noon, the weather had improved, although the winds remained high.

As we reached the end of the valley, we traversed a large area of low hills, ridges and mounds of loose rock, broken by water-filled pits. Brian explained that this was a moraine, left behind by a glacier, while the water-filled depressions represented encapsulated areas of snow and ice which had since melted. Nestled among the rocks were hemispherical cushions of moss campion, cheerful with their masses of purplish-pink flowers. Nearby, brightly blooming clumps of mountain heather danced in the wind.

Poor Brian! Carrying almost forty-five kilograms over these rocky ridges was not easy. I found I had to stop often to rest, and I knew he needed the break as well. When he stopped and sank to the ground with his pack on, he was like a turtle on its back. He couldn't move or turn over. He would undo the straps, and I would help him work free of his backpack. Then, when it was time to get up, I'd lie down on my pack and strap myself in, Brian would give me a push up, strap himself in, and I'd give him a boost. He soon ripped the legs out of his pants from straining so much. What a sight we both were!

The weather continued to clear, and we spent the rest of the day walking along the west side of the lake where we had tried unsuccessfully to land the day before,

*Moonrise over Upper Kangalaksiorvik Lake,
11:00 p.m.*

Ungava Lemming. This species is restricted to the tundra zone of the Quebec-Labrador Peninsula.

and then down a broad valley towards Upper Kangalaksiorvik Lake. Scattered caribou wandered the slopes in the distance.

Our campsite that night was behind a small knoll which protected the tent on two sides and shielded us somewhat from the wind. It was a cozy little spot with a beautiful view of turquoise Upper Kangalaksiorvik Lake nestled beneath the mountains. When the sun disappeared around 11:00 p.m. the temperature was only about five degrees Celsius, so I was glad when we finished our evening meal and were in the tent for the night.

The next morning was absolutely beautiful. By 3:00 a.m. the sun had already started to rise and, by 6:30, the tent was like an oven. It was such a contrast to the last couple of days. I found it unbelievable that it could be so warm this far north.

It seemed that we had camped in an area populated by lemmings, and we could hear them scurrying around under the floor of our tent in the early morning. We had a leisurely breakfast and watched as a lemming went about his business running in and out of his tunnels, waiting for any leftovers and wondering who these giants were who were camped in his living room!

As I was washing our breakfast dishes, Brian started to take down the tent. The pegs were out of the ground and he was just about to detach the fly. Suddenly an enormous gust of wind swept down off the mountains and snatched the tent from his hands. It tumbled about half a kilometre down over the hill towards a stream which flowed into the lake. I had never seen Brian run so fast! He caught up to it as it snagged on some willows near the bottom of the valley. Fortunately, we had purchased a good quality tent for the trip, and the only damage was a small tear in the fly which was easily repaired with duct tape. We decided that we would always take down the tent together from then on, so that we could both hold on to it in the event we experienced more of these monster gusts of wind. Losing the tent would have been disastrous, as temperatures can plummet rapidly this far north and, as we were above the tree line, there was nothing with which to build a shelter.

Later that morning we came to the braided channels of a small river which flowed into Upper Kangalaksiorvik Lake. To our west a vast green pasture, broken here and there by a clump of low willows, rose gradually towards a series of snow covered mountains. Small herds of caribou, probably numbering several hundred in total, grazed contentedly on the verdant grasses.

Nearby, we found our first sign of human habitation in the form of an ancient Inuit ruin. Although the purpose of this three metre long, oval ring of boulders was not immediately obvious, it once may have been roofed with skins to form a crude shelter.

Brian.

UPPER KANGALAKSIORVIK LAKE

At one time, the Inuit were found throughout this region, eking out an existence based on hunting and fishing. By the late 1700s, however, the Moravians had begun to establish a series of mission stations along the Labrador coast, including one at Ramah, south of Nachvak Fiord, in 1871, and at Killinek, near Cape Chidley, in 1905.

While the arrival of the Moravians, as well as contact with Newfoundland fishermen and traders, began a gradual process of conversion to Christianity and westernization, it also contributed to the depopulation of the region. The Inuit were repeatedly devastated by introduced diseases, particularly the influenza epidemic of 1918-19 which wiped out almost the entire population of some communities. The Moravians closed their mission station at Ramah in 1908 because of its isolation, and relocated the inhabitants to Hebron, a community which was itself resettled in 1959. Killinek was abandoned in 1925. Gradually all of the more northerly settlements in Labrador were abandoned, so that there is no longer a single permanent resident in the almost five hundred kilometres of coast between Nain and Cape Chidley.

The many channels made this river easy to cross, and it had a sandy bottom in the first few sections so that we didn't have to tackle the unstable rocks which characterize many rivers in the Torngats. The current was not fast, but the water was very cold and still came up to the bottom of my jacket. Brian was ahead of me, but had

31

to come back, as I was unsteady in the stream with my backpack on. The final section of this river did have rocks on the bottom, but was not deep. Brian slipped in the river and fell on one hand, but was unable to stand up with all the extra weight. After I helped him up, we decided we would always stay together when crossing streams. In some of the rivers we encountered later, we would have no choice.

Quite a bit of fine sand had washed into Brian's sneakers in crossing the river and, although he cleaned them out as well as he could, it was impossible to completely eliminate the sand from his socks and the foam lining of his sneakers. With the constant walking in wet socks and the abrasive action of the sand, he found his feet were blistered by the end of the day. While his feet didn't get a chance to heal properly for the duration of the trip, it didn't slow him down any. I also had problems with my feet at the end of the trip, but, thankfully, I had no blisters for the whole time.

We next faced a two hundred metre climb. We stopped about halfway up and had lunch, enjoying the warm breeze and the view of the lake and river valley below. In the distance we could see where we had camped the night before. As we ate lunch, I saw some movement out of the corner of my eye. It was a female willow ptarmigan moving between some rocks near the side of a small brook. She was so well camouflaged that we would never have seen her if she hadn't moved. A few moments later we saw a couple of chicks running along behind. They too blended perfectly with the rocks and, when not moving, were barely discernible, even though we knew they were there. We watched for a while without stirring. Soon, however, it was time to get moving again. As we started getting our packs back on, the ptarmigan slipped away between the rocks and disappeared.

The long climb to the plateau was very tiring with our heavy packs, and we rested often. As we climbed, we could see something silhouetted against the sky, and Brian said it was probably an Inukshuk. Inukshuk is an Inuktitut word meaning "like a person" (an Inuk). These compasses of the north are used even today by Inuit hunters to mark high points of land, good hunting and fishing grounds, or the route back home. The stones are set to resemble a human figure, and the manner in which they are placed gives direction or marks a trail on the tundra. We saw this Inukshuk from quite a distance away as it stood out against the sky. It was easy to see why they are used.

At the top of this rise was a large stony plain. The ground surface here seemed to have only recently thawed, and consisted mainly of loose rocks which more or less floated on a bed of saturated clay. This made walking difficult, as it would have been easy to twist an ankle trying to walk from rock to rock with all our gear. The large rocks and muddy ground also made the going very slow. It took us the rest of the day to cross this area and we were quite tired, but there was absolutely nowhere to

Inukshuk, south of Upper Kangalaksiorvik Lake.

Arctic Hare. These animals are surprisingly large, sometimes achieving a weight of more than five kilograms.

put up a tent. Finally, as we approached another small river, we found a spot among some huge rocks which was just large enough for the tent. It was a cozy little spot with a lovely view of the river below.

As we were putting up the tent, Brian motioned to me to be still and pointed out a curious arctic hare which was observing us from behind one of the rocks. He slowly got his camera ready, but the movement frightened the animal and he disappeared. While I cooked our meal, Brian kept an eye out for the hare and, sure enough, he returned to continue his investigation. Brian took several pictures before it decided to move on.

As we finished our evening meal (corned beef and macaroni fried up with onions) and got ready to settle in for the night, the deepening shadows accentuated the immensity and isolation of these northern mountains. Behind us, the rocky plateau rolled away to meet the skyline before dropping towards the Kangalaksiorvik Lakes. To our west, several kilometres away, there were a series of white-capped mountains. To the east, the monotony of this great plain of sedge and rock was broken only by Tower Mountain, which rose, cone-like, more than five hundred metres above the plateau. To the south, and more than ten kilometres distant, two huge pyramidal peaks stretched towards the sky, their snow covered sides bronze in the last rays of the setting sun.

CHAPTER 6

CROSSING THE RIVERS

T he next morning dawned clear and sunny. A short distance below us the river sparkled as it flowed over rocky shallows before hurling itself into a narrow, snow-roofed chasm. The snow bridge certainly looked like the easiest way to cross the river, and the thought of having to wade through icy-cold water so early in the morning held little appeal. However, we couldn't take a chance on breaking through and plunging into a gorge of rushing water. We decided to walk upriver a short distance and cross at a wider section. Although the current was not as deep, the rocks were large and unstable underfoot.

As we climbed up from the river valley, we expected the land to level out but, instead, it was a series of gently rolling ups and downs. As we walked, two snowy owls swooped low over the tundra. They kept their distance, occasionally perching on large rocks as they kept us in sight. When we reached the crest of the next ridge we realized why, as we could see a large quantity of loose, white feathers scattered across the hillside. We soon found a nest with two chicks, as well as two almost perfectly round, unhatched, white eggs. The newborn chicks still had their egg teeth in place, and were naked except for a fine coating of thin, white down. We were surprised to find the nest built on the ground, without protection from the weather or any effort at concealment. It seemed likely that the owls were probably well able to defend their nests from the foxes that roam these high barrens in search of food. After several quick photographs we hurried on so as not to upset the parents.

After a few more ups and downs, the land gradually levelled off. A short time later we saw an arctic fox peeping out at us over a small, sandy knoll. We watched as he came out in full view, and then noticed a second fox walking along the route we had just travelled, sniffing our tracks. After they entertained us for a few minutes with their sharp, dog-like yapping, we were on our way.

Ryans Bay more or less marks the northern end of the Torngats, with only a few mountains attaining heights in excess of 1,000 metres. As we moved south, however, the mountains became higher and increasingly dramatic,

Snowy Owl nest.

so that we were now approaching a number of peaks which were well in excess of 1,500 metres. I found distances very deceiving when surrounded by these enormous mountains. Sometimes, when a mountain came into view, we would still be looking at it after two days of walking. Indeed the mountains we had seen from our campsite the previous evening did not appear to be any closer at the end of the following day.

The word "Torngat" means "land of the devils" and Brian told me stories of the Inuit gods as we hiked along. Before the introduction of Christianity, and in fact well into the twentieth century in some cases, the Inuit believed that all phenomena and events were caused by the actions of spirits. The most powerful of these was the Torngak. An unfriendly god, the Torngak required constant appeasement through offerings of clothes and foodstuffs, and, when disgruntled, was apt to bring hardship through fierce storms and a variety of other misfortunes. The Inuit thought he was responsible for the monster winds that suddenly gust up, and that this happened when he was angry about something. I said a few words to him as we hiked along as I wasn't about to take any chances on getting on anyone's bad side. We needed all the friends we could get!

The legendary home of the Torngak was the Torngat Mountains. He was, however, merely the greatest of the spirits which inhabited this northern world. Tornarsuak, another great spirit who had taken the form of a giant polar bear, was thought to dwell in a cave somewhere between Cape Chidley and Nachvak Fiord, and controlled the actions of the sea animals. Brian told me that there was also a female goddess who had a more pleasant personality and who was responsible for the sun, soft winds and blue sky, so I talked to her a few times as well.

Later that day we crossed a broad valley, waded another river, and circled around the lower slopes of a large mountain. As we walked, we occasionally traversed large patches of snow that, in some cases, were a half kilometre or more long. The walking here was easy, as the snow was firmly packed and the necessity to place each step with caution to avoid loose rocks was temporarily eliminated. Large areas of these snowfields were a distinct pink colour, a phenomenon which Brian explained as being caused by bacteria feeding on wind-blown material which had mixed with the snow.

By now it was early evening and we were quite tired. Suddenly, just as it appeared that we would have to make camp in a seemingly limitless wasteland of rock and snow, we found a campsite that was like paradise. It appeared out of the blue as we navigated the side of a long slope overlooking the Komaktorvik River. A depression in the side of the hill hid a rivulet which formed a waterfall as it entered a tiny pond. The evening was calm and the pond like a mirror.

41

TREKKING THROUGH NORTHERN LABRADOR

We set up our tent next to the pond, on a small patch of sandy soil which had been washed down by the brook. Behind us was the soothing sound of the waterfall. We were on a ledge that overlooked a wide valley and river surrounded by mountains. The view was amazing, the weather was comfortable, and we even had our own private bath, albeit a little cold. This was one of my favourite campsites for the whole trip.

The next morning brought us to a swift river flowing out of the Komaktorvik Lakes. Here we saw signs of modern human activity. The remains of an old camp were surrounded by a quantity of fuel drums, several still full. We also found the remains of an inflatable boat, as well as pieces of a wooden freighter canoe. Scattered along the beach and among the crowberry bushes were a new outboard motor propeller, some shovels and pickaxes, and a variety of tools. Brian retrieved a pair of vise-grips which he added to his pack.

It was obvious that the site had not been used for years, and we surmised that it might have been an old prospecting camp. The lake would be an ideal landing spot for a plane, and the moraine at the end would provide some shelter for a camp. How it came to be abandoned remains a mystery, but I was saddened to see the effects of human activity on this lovely beach.

▸ *Campsite, overlooking Komaktorvik River.*

After exploring this area for a short time, we attempted to cross the river at a wide point that appeared more shallow than other areas. The current was fast, deep and very cold. We had read information regarding crossing mountain streams and now put this knowledge to the test. By starting downriver and working our way across on an upstream angle, we were able to lean into the current, thereby helping us to keep our balance. Our heavy packs helped to keep us from being swept off the bottom, and Brian would stand on my upstream side to break the current. It would have been impossible for a single person to cross such a boiling torrent, as he would be swept away as soon as one leg was lifted off the bottom to make another step. Consequently, we held hands to stabilize ourselves as we tried to cross, taking turns anchoring each other. We moved only a few centimetres at a time, making sure each foot was firmly wedged into the bottom of the river before moving forward with the other foot, and then waiting for the other person to move forward as well. It was a time-consuming, nerve-wracking undertaking.

On this attempt, when the water came up to the bottom of my jacket, the current became too strong and the water so cold that we both started to lose the feeling in our legs and feet. We were not far above a falls and were nervous about being swept downstream, so we turned back.

After scouting some distance up and down the

river, we made a second attempt, closer to the lake where the current appeared to be slower. This time the water was too deep. It was up to my armpits and the tent and sleeping pads were all under water. The water was numbingly cold, and again we were forced to turn back. The wind sweeping down across the lake was frigid, and we found shelter on the lee side of a moraine to try and get some warmth back in our bodies before trying another crossing point. I was beginning to feel very negative about making it across, but, one thing about this type of adventure, you couldn't turn around and go back! We had our lunch of a chocolate bar and fruit punch made from powdered crystals, and made one last attempt to cross.

We plotted a route which began not far from the site of our first attempt, crossing in a "V" pattern to avail of the shoal points. As we approached the middle, the water foamed around the bottom of my jacket, but did not appear to be getting any deeper. The current was still fast, and we took very cautious steps, only one person moving at a time, while holding hands to anchor each other. I was downstream from Brian so he absorbed most of the current and shielded me somewhat. I prayed I could keep enough strength in my legs to reach the opposite bank. It looked so far to the other side and getting across seemed to take a lifetime.

Determination and the basic need to survive kicks in at a time like this. It also made me more aware of how frightening this remote area could become if one of us had an accident or serious injury. This was not a place to take any chances! For just a moment while out in the middle of the river, I wondered what it would be like walking along a beach in Florida. Certainly much warmer! I have often said to Brian at times like this, "I wish sometimes we were like 'normal' people, taking simple, leisurely vacations." His response is always, "Why would you want to be 'normal'? 'Normal' is boring!"

Eventually the river became shallower, and we stumbled, numb and shivering, onto the far bank. From here we faced a long, five hundred metre climb through a mountain valley to reach a stream flowing out of Chasm Lake. The rise was fairly steep, and we had to rest many times because crossing the river had weakened our legs. Mine felt like jelly and were very shaky. The sun felt warmer by then (around 2:00 p.m.) and the wind, since it was no longer sweeping across the frigid water of the Komaktorvik Lakes, was not as cold. This helped dry our clothing and the outside of the tent.

We were tired, but not too tired to enjoy the scenery as we rested. It was beautiful looking down through the valley, with the sun shining on the snowcapped mountains as they swept up from the sides of the turquoise lakes. It gave me such a feeling of "getting away from it all". No phones, no hustle and bustle, no noise except for the breeze rustling through the grass on the side of the hill and the sound of waves lapping the shoreline of the lake. It was so tranquil and serene lying

Precipice Mountain,
elevation 1,200 metres.

off in the sun, we hated to get our packs back on and finish the climb.

When we reached the summit of the pass between the two valleys, we saw several rock ptarmigan with their chicks, as well as a number of small stones, left behind by the Inuit in days gone by as route markers. Behind us, Precipice Mountain loomed against the horizon. It is interesting to note that, in 1995, there was a muskox sighting near here, the first confirmed for Labrador.

We began to look for a campsite, but we had to walk for another hour and a half before we found somewhere that wasn't rocky and which was fairly close to water. Eventually we waded the stream which flowed down from Chasm Lake and camped on a small grassy meadow on the other side. I think that was our most exhausting day of the whole trip, and we were very glad to find a place to stop. It was much later than usual, and we only had a short time before the sun disappeared over the mountains. It was cold by the time we finished our meal and prepared to get in the tent for the night. It wasn't quite dark, and there was a lovely moon. In fact, we saw no real darkness until we were further south. It was never dark any night when we settled in and by 3:00 a.m. it was already fairly bright. We probably slept through the couple of hours of twilight each night.

CHAPTER 7

THE CARIBOU OF LABRADOR

We carried several bottles of fly dope but seldom needed it after we left Kuujjuaq. Although flies can be a real problem in much of Labrador, we had no trouble except for an occasional boggy area. The generally dry terrain and cool nighttime temperatures probably helped.

Most days we broke camp well before 9:00 a.m., and we often stopped around 4:00 p.m. if we found a suitable campsite, as we didn't want to take a chance on being stuck late in the day on a high, rocky plateau, with no potential camping places in sight for miles. Those days also gave us time to wash our clothes in a nearby brook and to put our facecloths and bars of soap to work! The water was too cold to bathe in, but we made the best of it.

49

TREKKING THROUGH NORTHERN LABRADOR

Our propane cylinders were heavy and in limited supply, and warming water for bathing was restricted to the lower river valleys where we could light a fire with some dry willows.

We saw hundreds of caribou as we travelled along, and it was sometimes difficult to find a spot to sit or put up the tent that did not include a smattering of droppings. Their trails up and down the valleys and across the tundra seemed endless. Often, these trails helped us find the best route, the caribou being much more knowledgeable of the terrain than we were!

The Labrador Peninsula is home to the George River caribou herd, the world's largest, with an estimated population of more than 500,000 animals. Labrador also contains a number of smaller herds, including one which lives in the Torngat region throughout the year. Since the George River herd migrates over great distances and includes the Torngat Mountains as a part of its summer range, it was uncertain whether we were seeing only the Torngat herd, or a portion of the George River herd as well.

In any case, the Torngats seem to provide an ideal summer breeding ground for these magnificent animals. The biting flies that are a scourge of wildlife in southern Labrador are largely absent, and predators are few. Meanwhile, the extensive glacial valleys filled with grassy turf provide abundant food.

THE CARIBOU OF LABRADOR

Except when accompanied by young, the caribou were quite tame and rather curious. Often they would approach quite closely when spoken to softly, or when attracted by a fluttering cloth or gently waving hand. Their eyesight is apparently quite poor, and Brian told me of an Inuit legend which says that the caribou once had large eyes and excellent eyesight. This made them difficult to hunt, and the Inuit prayed to their gods for help. Presently one of the caribou became thoughtful, and suggested to the others that they would be much better looking if their eyes were smaller. The other caribou agreed, and they sewed up their eyes with sinew, limiting their eyesight and making them easier to hunt. (Brian's stories were a constant source of entertainment throughout the trip.) There is no question the caribou rely on their keen sense of smell much more than their eyesight, and the more curious or suspicious among them would often circle around until they picked up our scent, after which they would bound off effortlessly over the tundra.

The next morning was sunny and warm and, after a leisurely breakfast of bacon, bannock and maple syrup, we packed up our gear and continued our walk up the side of the river flowing out of Chasm Lake. Although eight kilometres long, Chasm Lake never reaches a kilometre in width, forming a great gash in the heart of the mountains. On each side sheer cliffs rose more than 1,000 metres above the water. On the north side of the lake these cliffs culminated in an unnamed mountain of more than 1,600 metres. On the south side rose the twin peaks of Innuit Mountain and nearby Packard Mountain, both almost 1,700 metres in height. The steep mountains on each side of the lake were spectacular.

We turned off at the beginning of the lake and had an easy fifty metre climb to a plateau overlooking Nachvak Fiord. We were more than four hundred metres above sea level and could look out through the fiord and across to the massive cliffs of Kutyaupak Mountain on the other side. The talus slopes were a rich brown colour in the sun, and the brilliant blues of the sky and water were magnificent. We sat down and enjoyed the view before making our descent.

The land dropped away into nothingness before us and, while Brian had plotted a route on the map that appeared to allow for a safe, if steep, descent, we followed the caribou trails to ensure we picked the best route. At the bottom, we found an attractive campsite at the junction of two streams which ran into the fiord. It was a cozy little spot at the base of the mountain, surrounded by willows, alders, and dwarf birch. It was a quiet, peaceful spot to get cleaned up, wash clothes, have dinner, light a fire, and watch the sun go down.

The next morning we were awakened shortly after 5:00 a.m. by the sound of falling rocks, and we looked out to see a herd of about thirty-five or forty caribou coming down the valley we had descended the previous evening. We remained very still as they passed just behind our tent and out to the shoreline. Many of the animals were very young, and the mothers didn't like to come too close with their calves.

One thing that we found very strange that morning was that, when Brian went to the nearby stream where we had gotten our water the night before, it had completely dried up! There had been quite a lot of water in it the previous evening, and we had been forced to jump from rock to rock to get across. The dramatic change was a result of the heat of the sun causing a lot of snow to melt on the tops of the mountains during the day. Then, after the sun went down and the temperature dropped, the snow stopped melting and the smaller streams dried up. As our campsite was at the junction of two streams, we had no trouble getting water from the other, larger one.

There was a small delta at the mouth of the brook, formed by material washed downstream during spring floods or winter avalanches. Here we found a number of "tent rings", or circles of round stones. These were used by the Inuit to secure the edges of their tents, and were a sure sign of occupation in days gone by.

The abandoned Hudson's Bay Company post of Nachvak, or Kipsimarvik, was located in a small cove just to our east. The Inuit from as far away as eastern Ungava Bay used to trade there, travelling through the mountain passes and over the frozen lakes and bays in the winter months. Established in the 1860s, the post was incredibly

isolated and was visited by a company boat only once or twice each year. Although abandoned in the early 1900s, the foundations of this lonely post are still clearly visible, surrounded by a few Inuit graves.

From here we could look across Tasiuyak Arm and clearly see the valley which was to be our route to Tallek Arm. It looked so close, and yet we had to walk approximately eight kilometres along the shore to reach the end of Tasiuyak Arm, cross the Nachvak River, and then hike another five kilometres down the other side to get to the mountain valley we could now see.

◄ *Overlooking Nachvak Fiord.*
Kutyaupak Mountain rises more
than 1,000 metres in the background.

CHAPTER 8

THE NACHVAK RIVER

It was a sunny, still morning as we began our trek around the side of Nachvak Fiord, and the reflection of the mountains on the ocean, which was as smooth as a mirror, made a lovely start to the day. A seal sunned itself on a rock at the water's edge, and a flock of red-breasted mergansers scooted over the still water. I was amazed at the number of jellyfish washed up all along the shore. Many of them were very large, up to fifty centimetres across. Brian told me these were lion's mane jellyfish, so called for the colour of their bodies and long streams of reddish tendrils.

Nachvak Fiord is surrounded by thousand metre mountains which terminate in steep talus slopes, and Brian was concerned that picking a route might be difficult, or that, even worse, our way might be blocked by cliffs or rock outcroppings. Fortunately, these fears proved to be unfounded.

It was low tide when we started out, and it appeared that the action of the ice and the waves had left a narrow shelf just below the high water mark. This made for excellent walking on the sand and broken rock close to the edge of the water. As the tide came back in, however, we were forced back onto the unstable scree slopes at the base of the mountains. At one point we came to an area where there had been a massive landslide. Some of the rocks were the size of houses and it took some climbing to get over, and, in some cases, under them. As we couldn't see around them to the other side, we were hoping this didn't continue for too long. Luckily this proved to be the only major obstacle, and we were relieved to see the end of the Arm when we reached the other side of the landslide.

As we walked along, Brian pointed out garnets in some of the rocks which had fallen down off the mountains. While I had seen garnets before, they had always been a dull ruby-red colour. These, however, were bright lavender in colour and were invariably found in pieces of snow-white quartzite, making striking specimens.

By noon we had reached the Nachvak River, which we would have to cross before going down the other side

Labrador Tea. As the name suggests, the leaves can be steeped in hot water to make tea.

*A traditional Inuit grave,
Nachvak Fiord.*

of Tasiuyak Arm, and found a large, swift river. We now clearly faced the greatest challenge of our trip. We walked upstream to see if there was a wider section which might be more shallow, and found a spot where the river separated into two channels. We crossed the smaller channel very cautiously, anchoring each other as we went. The current was fast, cold and deep, but not unmanageable. We rested on an island between the two channels before attempting to cross the second.

We planned a route before we stepped into the water and held on to each other for support. This channel was by far the larger of the two and the water kept getting deeper and faster. We were less than halfway across when our legs became too cold and numb to fight the current any more. Brian was upstream and the current was splashing around the tops of his thighs like white water around a boulder in the middle of a rapid. We knew we had to turn around and go back, but it was difficult. When we were side-on, we were more streamlined in the current, and one leg shielded the other. However, when we tried to turn, the current would push against both legs and it was difficult to avoid being knocked off balance.

It took us a few moments to get turned around in the icy water. Brian stayed upstream to break the current, and I held on to his arm to steady myself as I slowly turned around. Then I positioned myself and Brian held on to me while he turned himself around. My legs were starting to weaken, and it took all my strength to lift each

THE NACHVAK RIVER

leg, fight the current, and force my foot back to the bottom. We collapsed when we made it back to the island.

As we slowly regained our strength, we saw several caribou coming down the side of the river. One was only a small calf. We watched as they crossed, the current flushing them downstream as they swam. The calf appeared to be a bit nervous and didn't go in the water. It's mother had already crossed and she walked back up the side of the river and swam back to the other side to retrieve her calf. This time they went into the water together. The little one washed quite a distance downstream before it made it to the other bank.

The cobble covered island we were on provided only a temporary resting place. We took our time crossing back to the north bank of the river, and were very glad to be out of the cold water. It was only about 2:00 p.m., but we agreed we were too tired to try again that day.

After we found a level spot among the willows and set up the tent, we had lunch and walked up as far as Nachvak Lake to scout for a better crossing point. The current appeared to be just as bad, or worse, as we approached the lake. We thought about walking up the side of the lake and crossing at the far end, but the shoreline slopes were very steep and the lake quite a few kilometres long. Eventually we decided we would make another attempt to cross somewhere in the same area the next day. Because of our experience with the stream that had dried up, we thought the river might drop a few centimetres overnight. Brian put a rock at the water's edge so that he could measure any change in the water level in the morning.

We had another lovely campsite. We were still at sea level with plenty of willows for shelter and firewood. Looking out the door of our tent we could see the river and, directly across from us, a massive, double-peaked mountain. Caribou trails meandered all along the slopes near the bottom. Brian walked out to the side of the river and called for me to come and watch more caribou coming down the river. We also saw a group of harlequin ducks riding the rapids. They certainly seemed to be having more fun out there than we did!

That night I didn't have much of an appetite as I had butterflies in my stomach in anticipation of what we would have to face the next morning. Brian suggested that, if we were unable to wade across, he would swim across with the packs and then come back for me. It wasn't a prospect I was looking forward to for many reasons, not the least of them the fact that I can't swim!

The next morning we checked the water level on our rock and found it had dropped slightly. We had had a nice, long rest during the night, so we forced down a quick breakfast and decided to try again. The water was just as cold and fast but, because the water level had dropped slightly and we were fresh and well rested, it was

Nachvak River.

somewhat easier to keep our balance.

We waded the first channel without too much difficulty and walked up to the top of the island before attempting to cross the second channel. Again, we took our time and, as we neared the middle of the river, we realized it wasn't getting any deeper. Our feet and legs were numb, but we gradually inched our way past the mid-point and the worst was over.

I know I said a lot of prayers on this trip. Although not much of a church goer in recent years, I grew up in a Christian home and still have the same beliefs I was taught as a child. I always felt we were being looked after on our trip and I said a quiet thank-you every time we got through a tough situation. I told Brian he'd better say a few prayers too, although I know a lot of our good fortune can be attributed to his strength, knowledge and research. At times when our maps weren't quite enough to guide us down a mountain, I believe the caribou trails were brought to our attention to help us descend safely.

After we had crossed, Brian admitted that he had been apprehensive about this river from the beginning, but had refrained from mentioning it as he did not want me to be worried. I'm not as brave as he! Even Brian, however, didn't expect it to be quite so difficult. It seemed likely that all the warm weather over the previous few days had caused the snow on the mountains to melt much faster than usual, raising the water levels of the lakes and rivers. Based on the width of some of the river beds, one could only imagine what some of these rivers would be like during the spring run-off when they were in flood.

Caribou stags, near Nachvak Fiord.

CHAPTER 9

BLACK BEARS

Whered we finally reached the other side of Nachvak Brook, we dropped our packs and stumbled around the crowberry heath as we tried to restore feeling to our numb limbs. Our legs pained terribly from the deep, frigid water, but the day was warm and we soon got our circulation going. There were many signs of Inuit habitation on the south side of the river in the form of tent rings and the remains of stone caches that had once been used to store dried arctic char.

Walking down the south side of the Arm was relatively easy. At one point, as we rested on the bank, we were surprised to see a large seal swimming underneath the clear, green water below us. After about five kilometres, we left Tasiuyak Arm and began a long climb (a bit of a "grunt" as Brian called it) to a three hundred metre high pass that would take us to Tallek Arm, the southern extension of Nachvak Fiord. It was already after 5:00 p.m., and we were anxious to set up camp as soon as we found a suitable place.

The route down to Tallek Arm was fairly steep, and the action of the frost had left many loose rocks. We had to take our steps very carefully. Brian was a short distance ahead and, when I looked up, I saw two large black bears on a rocky hummock just to his right. Brian had been concentrating on his footing and, even though the bears were only a few metres away, he had not yet seen them. I shouted a warning, and he struck his metal ammunition/camera case on a boulder to frighten them off. One turned away, but the other looked as if he was searching for something appetizing, like us, for his dinner! Brian shouted and waved his arms, but this only made them more curious.

As they began to amble towards us, their tan muzzles sniffing the air, Brian struggled with the rusty zipper of his gun case. I knew that he would have preferred to take out his camera, but these bears were just too close for comfort. They were still advancing as Brian finally managed to assemble and load the rifle. He fired a shot over their heads and, much to our relief, they quickly disappeared from view into some nearby willows.

Brian later told me black bears do not normally

live above the tree line, and that the substantial numbers found in the Torngat Mountains and around Hebron Fiord, further south, are an unusual occurrence which is of considerable interest to biologists. These bears are also unusually large, perhaps reflecting greater dependence on meat as a source of food!

Our experience with the bears had made me nervous, and it was with considerable caution that we worked our way through a broad swath of head-high willows before reaching Tallek Arm. After breaking out on the shoreline, we walked along the edge of a two kilometre wide alluvial fan of loose boulders which had been swept down from a valley on our right. We kept close to the water so that the incoming tide would cover our tracks, just in case the bears were curious enough to follow us.

Camp that night was among the bushes at the base of a mountain near the end of Tallek Arm - a beautiful, peaceful place to watch the sun go down. There was no wind that evening and the surface of the water provided a perfect reflection of the massive cliffs above. Dead willow branches were plentiful and we enjoyed a lovely campfire. By bedtime, I had long forgotten the bears, but Brian later confessed to having spent a restless night, with every rustling of the willows conjuring up images of increasingly large and hungry bears!

The next morning we had a four kilometre walk

around the side of Tallek Arm before reaching the broad delta of the Palmer River. The river was braided into several channels, which cut down on the current and depth, and we were able to cross without any problems.

The Palmer River, like many of the geographical features of the Nachvak region, was named by the Brown-Harvard Expedition of 1900. Thus, Delabarre Bay, just south of the entrance to Nachvak Fiord, was named for Dr. Edmund B. Delabarre, the leader of the Expedition, while Cape Daly and Adams Lake were named for Reginald Daly and Huntington Adams respectively. Professor Packard and President Faunce of Brown University both had mountains named in their honour, as did President Eliot of Harvard. Mount Ford was named for George Ford, the Hudson's Bay Company's post manager at Nachvak. Ironically, Bigelow Bay, Bigelow Bight and the McCornick River were named for two undergraduate members of the Expedition who were never anywhere near the Torngats, having remained behind at Port Manvers, just north of Nain, until the Expedition's return.

Once we reached the east side of the Palmer, we followed the river valley upstream for about eight kilometres before coming to a small stream cascading down the mountains. This marked the route for our next climb. It would be more than seven hundred metres, so we decided to camp near the bottom in order to start fresh in the morning. We soon found a suitable spot in the form of a shallow depression next to the stream, in the process flushing a red fox who ran off over the boulders.

We had stopped a little earlier than usual, so we washed some clothes - and ourselves. Brian had inflated the camp rests and arranged the sleeping bags, and was soon sprawled face down in the tent, asleep. He looked comical with his feet protruding through the open door of the tent, one arm stretched out to each side, with his coat and woolen cap still on. I decided to take his picture and had the camera up to my face when I heard a rushing sound off to my right. I looked up and came face to face with an enormous black bear bouncing down over the side of the depression which sheltered our tent. He was very close, but I don't know who got the biggest fright! He wasn't expecting to see me, and he skidded to a stop before scrambling off in the other direction. I called to Brian quietly and told him we had company.

Brian was still groggy with sleep, but stumbled from the tent and up the knoll to see if the bear was still close by. In the meantime the bear had circled around and was now peering at me from behind the tent. After a number of shouts by Brian and me, it again retreated up over the knoll with a still disoriented Brian in hot pursuit. I called to him to suggest that, if he were planning to chase black bears over the tundra, it might be advisable to take the gun. This struck Brian as a reasonable suggestion and, after returning for the gun, he again climbed the knoll. He found the bear shuffling off in the other direction, but he fired the gun over its head to encourage it to keep going. Brian said that the smell of food cooking was very strong as it rose over the top of the knoll and that was probably what had attracted the bear. I was a bit nervous at this point. All I could think of was the fact that we had now seen three bears in two days. I wondered how many bullets we had with us, and hoped we weren't going to have to go through this on a regular basis. What if we ran out of bullets and ran into a nasty black bear or a polar bear? My imagination was getting the better of me.

The depression in which we had our tent was about fifty metres above the Palmer, so we could watch as the bear made his way down to the side of the river before heading toward Tallek Arm. We had a lovely view of the valley and out through the Arm, and I felt relatively comfortable knowing the bear was a safe distance from us. We slept well that night, but weren't looking forward to the long climb facing us. We expected it would take most of the next day.

It was cloudy in the morning and we slept until 8:00 a.m. I had wrenched my ankle a little the day before while walking over the loose rocks along the side of the Arm. It had bothered me all day, and I hoped it wouldn't act up on the long climb.

The route along the side of the stream was very steep and largely over broken rock, and we had to stop quite a few times on the way up. The climb offered spectacular views of Tallek Arm and, as we lay back enjoying the scenery, we saw a herd of caribou coming up through the notch below us. The animals didn't notice us at first, and some of them came quite close. I started to count them as they passed but gave up after one hundred. One poor thing only had three legs. We wondered what could have caused such a terrible injury. Whatever had happened, it was able to hop along quite successfully on its one hind leg. I wished I could climb these mountains as well as it could.

By 3:30 p.m. we had crossed the still frozen surface of the lake that effectively marked the top of the pass, and started looking for a place to set up camp. These high plateaus were not ideal camping places as they were usually rocky with very little shelter. We were quite tired after the long climb, but had to walk several more kilometres before finding shelter on a small area of turf next to some low bedrock outcrops. We dropped our packs and gratefully set up the tent. Because we were at a higher elevation, we had the sun for much longer than usual before it disappeared behind the mountains. We would be heading down to the valley of the Korok River the next day.

That night, as we lay in our sleeping bags, we were actually in Quebec, having just crossed over the "height of land" that marks the boundary between that province and Newfoundland and Labrador. Here, the

Overlooking Tallek Arm.

forces of erosion were hard at work, and we were awakened several times throughout the night by the rumble of rock slides tumbling off the sides of the mountains that surrounded us.

CHAPTER 10

THE KOROK RIVER

T he next morning was calm and brilliantly clear, the heat driving us from our tent by 6:00 a.m. The weather had now been warm and sunny, with no rain, for more than a week.

Just to the east lay the true heart of the Torngats, with a number of peaks exceeding 1,500 metres, the highest in mainland Canada east of the Rockies. These mountains are truly wild, with sheer cliffs rising from a collection of small glaciers which are still actively carrying away their loads of rock and ice for deposition at lower elevations.

Remarkably, so remote and inaccessible is this part of the Torngats that they were largely overlooked by early explorers, and their true status has only recently become evident. Thus it was that Ron Wilson and Ray Chipeniuk, in making the first Canadian ascent of Torngarsoak Mountain in 1977, then thought to be the highest peak in Labrador at approximately 1,595 metres, gradually became aware of a significantly higher mountain nearby.

In 1978, Chipeniuk and Wilson, accompanied by five other members of the Alpine Club of Canada, returned to the Torngats where they successfully climbed the knife-edged peak they had seen the previous year. This mountain, which helps define the border between Newfoundland and Quebec in keeping with the "height of land" definition, has two distinct summits. The lower of these, lying entirely within Quebec and the highest point in that province at 1,622 metres, had already been named Mont d'Iberville by the Government of Quebec. The somewhat higher second summit, with an estimated height of 1,652 metres, was found to lie entirely within the boundaries of Newfoundland and Labrador. This peak was subsequently named Mount Caubvick, after an Inuit woman who was brought from Labrador to England in 1773 by George Cartwright, an explorer and trader who established trading posts and fishing and trapping operations at Cape Charles and Sandwich Bay in the late eighteenth century.

Unfortunately, the beautiful weather that we experienced early in the morning did not last and, as we approached the Korok River, ominous black clouds began

This is one of the longest of several small glaciers scattered throughout the Torngats. The flow of this glacier is clearly evident.

◄ *Meltwater stream atop a glacier in the Torngats. Debris at the base of such streams may eventually be left as long, winding ridges, called eskers, when the glacier melts.*

to roll down the mountains. We could see the showers coming and decided to cross the river before the rain started. We were about halfway across when the bottom came out of the sky. Thunder reverberated off the hills, while lightning crackled on all sides as the rain hit the river like icy black bullets. Although a sizeable river, the Korok was wide and relatively shallow, and not a hard river to cross at this point. The deepest part was just above my knee and the current was not fast. We were soaked, however, by the time we reached the other side.

Getting our legs and feet wet in the brooks and streams was a natural part of each day, but in a heavy rain, everything got wet from our head down, including the sleeping pads which were strapped to the outside of my pack. Although it was only 3:00 p.m. it was almost dark, and the rain showed no signs of letting up. We found a level, grassy spot behind a moraine, put up the tent, threw in our packs, and jumped in behind.

The moraine provided great shelter in what turned out to be a huge thunder and lightning storm. I crawled out of the tent around 8:00 p.m. and got hot chocolate and some crackers and cheese which served as lunch/dinner combined. It was still raining lightly and, just as I got settled back in the tent, it poured again, lasting throughout the night. I was glad to be in our warm, dry tent with dry clothes. We were fortunate to keep these dry throughout the trip. Our sleeping bags were in separate waterproof bags at the top of our packs for protection in case of rain or deep river crossings, and our clothes was all double bagged for the same reason.

Every evening, when we were in the tent for the night, we would write in our diaries, mark off the route we had taken, and plot our course for the following day. Brian always told me what to expect with respect to the type of terrain, the duration of our climbs, and the difficulty of the rivers and streams according to the maps. He was very accurate in his predictions.

On days like this when we stopped early, we had lots of time to nap and relax. We took advantage of these times to study our maps and write in our journals in more detail. My journal was the same one I carried on our vacation the previous July. That vacation was also our honeymoon. I got into the habit of recording our day's activities and then reading aloud to Brian where we had been the previous year on the same day. It was very interesting, as we had camped across the Northwest Territories, the Yukon and parts of Alaska. It was a wonderful trip, and it was very relaxing to read about it each evening after we were in the tent and settled away for the night.

By 6:30 the next morning the sun had started to burn off the fog and mist, and Brian threw some of our wet things over the tent to dry. The air temperature was very warm, even though the fog lingered over the tops of the mountains and there were more black clouds

approaching. We kept watching the weather, and I knew in the back of my mind that this could not be a leisurely trip. We had a deadline for pickup by plane and were always concerned that the weather might take a turn for the worse. Our early stop the day before had put us slightly behind schedule.

We had some pancakes and the last of our bacon for breakfast and packed up around 8:00 a.m. We would have a walk of about fourteen kilometres up the south side of the Korok before reaching the valley that would take us back across the Quebec-Newfoundland border and to our food drop in the next river valley.

The sun stayed out for a while and it was uncomfortably warm and muggy. Soon, however, the clouds rolled back in with showers of cold rain. The walking was very good until we came to a boggy area at a bend in the river. After all the rain, it was not ideal walking conditions. While Brian had no problem walking through the spongy bog with his long legs and six foot plus height, I found it much more difficult with my short legs, especially with a backpack.

By the time we reached the end of the bog, the winds had picked up dramatically and we were enveloped in a cold fog. We found a sheltered spot at the base of a

◄ *The Korok River, Quebec.*

cliff surrounded by snowbanks, and managed to get the tent up before the rain became too heavy.

Days like this were miserable, and preparing a hot meal in the cold rain and wind was next to impossible. We had had little to eat the day before, and the prospects for dinner today didn't look promising. We carried a few crackers, cheese, jam and some mixed nuts and raisins for times like this. One thing in our favour was that we were so tired at the end of the day that we had no trouble sleeping, no matter how early we stopped.

CHAPTER 11

REACHING OUR FOOD DROP

T he next day was Thursday, July 28, and we had only five full days left. By this time I was starting to get a bit nervous about our schedule. We didn't want to allow for any hiking time on August 2, as we would need to be at the pickup point fairly early in the morning.

Brian had planned our itinerary before we left, but he adjusted the route some evenings according to the weather and walking conditions, taking into account the timing and difficulty of climbs. We had planned to take a few side trips, and Brian had wanted to climb to the summit of some of the mountains. We thought we could set up a base camp where we would leave our supplies, hike to the tops of the mountains, and return to camp in the evening. After a few days walking, however, we

Alpine flowers. The flowers of northern Labrador have adapted to the climate in a variety of ways. Most are on exposures facing the sun, and the bright flowers and low, bushy nature of most plants help to maintain warmth.

decided to stick with the main route and not take on any extra mileage. Brian knew I didn't like extensive climbing, and one evening as we were marking off our route for the next day, he told me he had adjusted our route to avoid a thousand metre climb. I was so relieved, I didn't care that it might add on a few extra kilometres. We had been walking for almost two full weeks and were starting to feel the effects. A climb of a thousand metres with a heavy backpack was not very appealing, even to Brian.

We had also planned to visit the former Moravian mission site at Ramah before swinging back around past our food drop. However, the weather over the last couple of days had slowed us down somewhat, so we decided to head straight up through a south trending valley at the head of the Korok River and down to the lake where our food was.

It had rained heavily throughout the night but, when we awoke on the morning of our thirteenth day, we were grateful to find it had finally stopped. The sun came out while we had a pancake breakfast. There were still some dark clouds lingering, but we packed up and set out to continue our journey.

We had camped just before an area where the Korok flowed out through a steep, narrow valley, hemmed in on both sides by high mountains. This gorge-like valley was approximately a kilometre in length, and we went only a short distance before coming to an immense snowbank that fell almost vertically from the face of the cliffs above us. The snowbank was at least a hundred metres across and was undercut from below by the swift waters of the Korok. It was an uncomfortable place to be, but we kicked footholds in the firm snow and gingerly made our way across.

Before long the gorge was behind us, and I found an old rusty trap as we crossed a series of broad sand flats at the head of the Korok. We now faced a four hundred metre climb up to the next valley. The first one hundred metres were very steep, and we stopped quite often. As we rested, we could see a large black bear peering intently into the water as he sat on his haunches by the side of the river. Whether he was fishing or simply admiring his reflection is impossible to say!

By now Brian's pack was much lighter, as our food had been reduced quite a bit, but the continued exertion and low food intake of the past few days had drained our energy. Eventually, however, we reached the summit of the pass, and we hoped to get to the lake where our food bag had been left before stopping for the day. Considering our meagre evening meals over the last couple of days, Brian was especially looking forward to his homemade french fries. Unfortunately, it started to rain heavily as the lake came into sight, and we had to stop early and set up camp in a sheltered but lumpy depression on the side of a hill. We were still several kilometres from our food.

Eventually the rain slackened for a few minutes and we got out of the tent and heated a pot of water for some soup. We had heard a small bird chirping anxiously while we were waiting for the rain to stop, and Brian soon found a savannah sparrow's nest with four eggs in it. Although quite close to the tent, it was well hidden under some low bushes of dwarf birch.

Because we had changed our minds about going to Ramah, retrieving our food would require a detour of several kilometres. I suggested to Brian that we forget about it, as the weather seemed to have taken a turn for the worse and we didn't want to lose any more time than we had to. It was still a considerable distance to North Arm, and getting our food would add on another half day. I felt we had enough provisions to stretch over the next four days, and there was always the possibility that animals had discovered our food and destroyed it anyway.

No way was Brian going to leave without getting his fries, beer and soft drinks ! My feet were starting to bother me by this time. They weren't blistered, but they were very tender from all the rough ground and constant pounding. Brian suggested we walk to the western end of the lake where I would stay with the gear while he went to pick up the food. He thought it wouldn't take him very long to do the six kilometre round trip without a pack. I didn't like the idea of Brian being gone for a couple of

Savannah Sparrow nest.

◄   *A ten metre high snowdrift calves*
    mini icebergs into an unnamed lake
    north of Nakvak Brook.

hours by himself, and I had visions of him being attacked by animals that might be lingering around the food. Of course, I wasn't keen on being alone for any length of time either.

The next morning it was still raining lightly. We waited for a while and then decided to pack up and get moving. Cooking breakfast in the cold rain held little appeal, and we decided we would wait until we got to the extra food before we ate.

It was a cold, gusty morning when we reached the lake, but at least the rain had stopped. We dropped our gear and, since I did not want to be left alone, started towards the food drop. As we walked we occasionally had to climb over huge snowdrifts, some more than ten metres high, that extended out into the lake. In places large pieces had broken off, like icebergs from a glacier.

After about a kilometre, we came to a somewhat higher area which offered a good view of the rest of the lake. Brian suggested I stay there, since he wouldn't be out of sight for more than a few minutes. I agreed, reluctantly, to let him go on alone and waited as he walked towards the end of the lake. It seemed like forever, even though it was only a little over two kilometres. There were a few scattered ravines leading into the lake, and he would occasionally drop out of sight for a few minutes. I started to think about polar bears and wolves, so I loaded the gun and sat down with it laid across my knees. I must have looked like a female Davy Crockett!

As Brian gradually disappeared in the distance, I hoped he would not run into any trouble. I had enough faith in his mapping skills and sense of direction to know that his calculation on the exact location of the food was very accurate. However, it seemed like a lifetime waiting for him to reappear. Then I saw him! He was carrying the big, bright orange bag over his shoulder. The bag was fairly heavy, and I could see he was having trouble carrying it, as there were no shoulder straps. He kept switching positions but it appeared to be in one piece. When he reached me, he rested before we set out on the walk back to our gear.

When we reached our packs, we opened the food bag and took out our new supplies. In addition to our much anticipated bag of potatoes and cans of beer and soft drinks, we had onions, carrots, dried peas, macaroni, salt pork, bacon, corned beef, crackers, bars, and cheese; not to mention a sizeable vacuum sealed package of salt riblets. There were also new containers of propane and paper towels. We were just like kids at Christmas. We drank our soft drinks while I heated the cooking oil on our small propane burner and cut up the potatoes for french fries. We cooked just about all the potatoes, saving only a couple to eat as pan fries with our new supply of bacon. We had our cans of beer with the fries. It was the best meal we had had in days!

We wanted to eliminate any extra weight, so we lit a fire and burned any garbage we had, as well as the plastic food bag. Our food bag had contained another large package of pancake mix, but we were so sick of pancakes by this time that we decided to burn it. We still had some of our original supply of pancake mix, and had used up all our syrup anyway. We had also been cooking with lard up to this point, and I hated it. There was a container of margarine in the food pack, so we decided to burn the lard as well. I was glad to see it disappear.

CHAPTER 12

NAKVAK BROOK

It was after mid-day by the time we got everything properly stored away in our packs. We had some moving around to do to accommodate the extra food, but it wasn't a real problem as we were only replacing some of the supplies we had in the beginning. Brian's pack still wasn't as heavy as it had been during the first few days.

We wanted to get a few more kilometres in for the day, as we really hadn't made much progress up to this point. I was beginning to feel very tired and my feet were bothering me. I had also been favouring the ankle that I had twisted a few days before. Although it wasn't too bad, the constant walking hadn't given it a chance to heal. After one hundred and sixty kilometres of walking, it probably wasn't surprising that my feet and ankles would give me some trouble.

I had to rest often that day and was glad we were getting closer to our pickup point. There was one more river between us and our destination, and Brian wanted to get as close to it as possible before we stopped for the day, as we found it was easier to cross the rivers early in the morning.

By about 6:00 p.m. we were both very tired. We had reached the beginning of the drop down to the river valley, but the decline consisted of a series of small plateaus, and we couldn't see the river. It was beginning to get cold and misty, with a stiff breeze blowing, so we stopped by a stream in a lovely sheltered area among the willows. We had a filling dinner of tinned corned beef and macaroni, fried up with onions, and lit a nice fire before we went to bed for the night.

The next morning was windy and cool, but the sun was shining. We cooked bacon and pan fried a couple of our potatoes for breakfast, and hoped the wet weather of the past few days was behind us.

We were both a little nervous about the river we were about to cross. Although called Nakvak Brook, it was actually a fairly substantial river. Brian expected it to be our last major hurdle before we reached North Arm in Saglek Fiord.

NAKVAK BROOK

As we followed some gravelly caribou trails upstream looking for a place to cross, Brian found a large piece of "Ramah chert". Chert is a hard, fine grained mineral that can be readily worked into a variety of sharp-edged tools or weapons. The chert found at Ramah is of a distinctive translucent gray colour, and was particularly prized for its quality. There is evidence that it was traded over astonishing distances, with specimens being recovered from aboriginal sites as far away as the eastern United States. The piece that Brian found was lying loosely upon the ground, and appeared to have been dropped by some prehistoric traveller.

Before long we reached an area where the river was wider and broken by several small islands. Here the current was a little slower and the water a fairly comfortable depth. Although we still had to support each other, it wasn't nearly as bad as some of the other rivers we had crossed.

It seemed that the caribou crossed this river in great numbers, and both banks were lined with thick windrows of matted hair. The caribou, like many animals in the north, grow an extra layer of fur in the fall which they shed in the warmer months, and the current had evidently washed away large clumps as they crossed.

As we walked along the south side of the river, we saw several flocks of ducks and geese in the steadies. We were glad we had crossed when we did, however, as the river soon narrowed and became much faster, and we could see from the map that there were several large falls further upstream.

The map also indicated we were about to enter a wooded area along the sides of the river. We were quite looking forward to this, as, with the exception of this one small area, our maps showed no trees anywhere else in the Torngats. In fact the nearest forested area that we knew of was in the lower reaches of the Korok River, well to our west. However, this so-called wooded area soon turned out to be nothing more than the product of some cartographer's overactive imagination, as we found nothing more than an unusually lush growth of head-high willows, alders and dwarf birch. Growing conditions here seemed to be particularly favourable, and the open spaces between the thickets contained partridgeberries and wild currants. In the damp areas we found our first cloudberries, or bakeapples as they are called in Newfoundland and Labrador.

As we walked through these thick clumps of vegetation, we were suddenly startled by a medium sized black bear. He had been lying down under one of the bushes and exploded to life at our feet. He was still shedding his winter coat and, as he disappeared, large clumps of reddish-black fur wafted through the air behind him. Judging by his speed, I think we frightened him almost as much as he frightened us. I can't say that I blame him, as we were looking very rough by this time!

NAKVAK BROOK

By 4:00 p.m. more cloud had moved in and we knew we were going to have another rainy evening. We found a sheltered spot among the bushes and battened down for what would turn out to be a very nasty rain and wind storm. Dinner consisted of a few nuts and some crackers and jam, as the weather was too miserable to cook anything outside. We were nice and cozy in the tent though. We had lots of time to check our maps and plot our route for the final leg of our trip. We expected to get to the falls early the next day.

The tent was buffetted by hurricane-force winds throughout the night, and we slept very little. I was nervous about the tent being able to take the pounding, but we stayed warm and dry inside. By morning the winds had subsided somewhat and the rain had stopped. We were able to enjoy a good "stick to your ribs" breakfast of bacon and the last of our pan-fried potatoes before setting out towards the falls.

The next couple of kilometres were very hard going, as the area consisted mainly of black bedrock outcroppings, with a lot of ups and downs. After a while we could hear the falls, but couldn't see them, as we had to keep back from the river in order to climb over some of these areas of rough bedrock.

The falls were only about three kilometres upstream from our last camping spot, but, by the time we got to a point where we could see the spray in the distance, I was very tired. I debated whether to climb down over the rocks, towards the falls on our right, or head off to the left towards our destination. Of course, Brian soon persuaded me to check out the falls. We left our gear and clambered out over the rocks. The land dropped off quickly, and we didn't have to go very far before we had them in view.

We sat for a few minutes, taking in the view and listening to the roar of the water. I was amazed by the volume of water going over the falls, and by the spray which rose high into the air from the foaming waters at their base. The land on the other side of the falls was rocky also, but the mist from the falls had left the vegetation a brilliant emerald green. The sky was a very deep blue. Times like this made me forget my sore feet and tired muscles. This was what it was all about.

After leaving the falls we climbed two hundred metres to a plateau that would take us across to a valley leading out to North Arm. The climb was not difficult and it was fairly pleasant with the sun shining, despite the cold wind. A couple of hawks screamed overhead.

As we continued across the plateau, the landscape gradually changed to a series of rolling ridges and shallow depressions. It was about ten kilometres across the top, and, after a few hours walking, I got very bored with the same surroundings. Although we knew we should be getting closer to the next valley, the scenery didn't change at all. We just walked from one low rocky ridge to the next. The sky had become overcast, and the distant mountains soon disappeared into the gray cloud.

As we approached the top of each ridge, we hoped we would see where the land started to drop off, but there was always another depression and another ridge behind it. The only change in the monotonous surroundings was the occasional area of wet clay. I went to my shins in one of these at about 4:30 and my aching feet got stuck. I just stood there and cried. I was so exhausted! Brian came back and, after taking my camera case and small backpack that I carried in my hand, helped me out of my predicament. We stopped at the top of the next ridge, enveloped in a gray world of rock and sky. There was nothing but the same countryside ahead of us.

We decided to stop for the night in the next depression. There wasn't a lot of shelter, but there was a small stream nearby and a level spot next to a bank which provided some protection for the tent. The wind was very cold as we ate our evening meal and, by the time I had finished putting away the dishes, my hands were frozen.

Brian was fed up with my whining by the time we got in the tent for the night. Poor thing, he was cold and tired too. While I was cooking dinner he went to fetch a pot of water and, when I looked at him, he had the leg of his pants torn from the crotch to below the knee. He hadn't shaved for more than two weeks and had lost quite a few pounds since we started this trip. He looked absolutely pathetic. He never complained about anything. His feet had been blistered since the third day, but he loves this country so much that he would have gone through just about anything to see as much of it as he could.

▸ *Falls on Nakvak Brook.*

CHAPTER 13

SNOWBOUND!

The next morning marked the start of our seventeenth day. We were supposed to be at the pickup point early the following morning, but we awoke to a cold, dreary rain, mixed with snow and sleet. When we peeped out the tent door, we could see the squalls sweeping over the tops of the mountains, the distant hills gradually whitening as they assumed their mantle of freshly fallen show.

We decided to nap for a while and hoped that it would ease off before too long. My feet and ankles had just about had it by this time, and a few extra hours of rest were just what I needed. We managed to boil some water for tea and took some nuts, crackers and jam into the tent for breakfast. The damp weather of the last couple of days had not been conducive to getting a thorough wash and we were both quite grubby. We smelled like two wet dogs.

By noon we were forced to decide whether we would pack up and start out in the squalls of sleet and wet snow, or stay put in the hope that the weather would improve by the next morning. We would be pushing it, but we didn't think the going would be too rough as we had no major uphill climbs and were only about twelve kilometres from the pickup point. The earliest possible arrival time for the plane would be about 9:00 a.m. and, with an early start, we would be there by then.

We looked out of the tent several times after lunch, but the squalls of sleet and snow continued throughout the day. There did not appear to be any sign of clearing. As a matter of fact, it worsened as the day progressed. We decided to settle in and get some well needed rest. We were nice and cozy in the tent. It was too miserable to cook, so we had some crackers, cheese and salami for dinner. We had had a good meal the day before and, since we weren't using any energy, we found we weren't all that hungry.

The next morning we were up at 4:00 a.m. Outside was a gray dawn, cold and windy with snow squalls, and we had to wear our woolen caps and mittens as we packed up our gear. Time was running out. We had only five hours to complete the remaining twelve kilometres to the pickup point.

We set out to finish the remainder of the endless plateau that we had started to cross two days before. In no time we could see the valley approaching. There was only one problem! When we reached the point where we were to begin our descent, we saw only jagged cliffs all the way to the bottom, with nowhere in sight to climb down. We continued to scout along the edge in the direction we were supposed to go, but there seemed to be no break in the sheer cliffs. We decided to backtrack to see if we could find a way down. We were losing a lot of time and getting nervous.

After a kilometre or so, we saw some caribou tracks leading out to the edge of the cliff. We followed them and found that, although the descent was very steep, there seemed to be a path that the caribou took to get down to the valley. This was not where we would have chosen to descend four hundred metres, but time was running out. Because of the steepness, we couldn't see the bottom, and we hoped that, when we came to the first ledge, we could find a way to the next one. If the cliff was straight down beyond the first ledge, we would have to climb back to the top again.

We eased our way cautiously down over the wet rocks, at times sitting and sliding while we used our feet for brakes, as a slip could be fatal. We had to pick our route carefully, following the path worn by the caribou

Caribou antlers.

hooves. The cliff was almost vertical, and we worked our way from ledge to ledge in a zig-zag pattern in order to get down safely. With our heavy backpacks, it would have been easy to lose our balance, and we had to continually shift our other gear back and forth as we sought to obtain secure handholds in the rock.

About halfway down, the sheer cliffs began to give way to steep slopes of loose talus, and we could see the waters of a small stream which flowed out into North Arm. It was still slow going, as the rocks were very unstable, and, by the time we reached the bottom, our legs were weak from the strain of the descent. Unfortunately, we could not rest as we had lost a lot of valuable time. We still had about nine kilometres to go.

CHAPTER 14

NORTH ARM

The stream at the bottom was initially quite narrow and filled with large quantities of loose rubble which had been washed down from higher levels. To make matters worse, the valley was choked with a dense growth of alders and willows, which slowed our progress considerably. After a couple of kilometres, however, the valley swung away to the right and broadened out into a series of grassy meadows.

An unusual characteristic of these meadows was the presence of large, isolated blocks of rock that were perhaps several stories in height. The area around these monoliths had been built up by outwash deposits from the stream and was now covered with a flat carpet of lush grass. It gave the whole area the appearance of a vast natural Stonehenge.

Soon the lake which we had designated as our pickup point was clearly visible. We had pushed ourselves hard to make sure we reached it before the plane's earliest expected arrival time and now, with the lake close at hand and no plane in sight, we were able to relax a little and enjoy a much needed breather.

As the morning progressed the weather underwent a dramatic improvement. The snow had stopped during our descent from the plateau, but we were too busy to notice. It wasn't as cold down in the valley, and then the sun came out. Another half hour brought us to the lake and, within a short while, we had skirted its western shore and forded the stream at its runout, gratefully dropping our packs in a grassy hollow on the other side.

After a short rest, we set out to explore our surroundings. There was a broad sandy beach at the south end of the lake, backed by a long sand dune. The dune was capped by a thick growth of willows, and we walked through to the other side, in the process flushing several coveys of ptarmigan. Here, in the shelter provided by the dune and the willows, it was absolutely beautiful. Mountains rose on both sides of us to a height of more than a thousand metres, the turquoise lake lay behind us and, beyond another area of willows, there was the ocean at North Arm. There was no wind on this side of the dune, and the sun was by now quite hot. We peeled off a few layers of clothes and lay off in the sun. It felt like heaven.

After a few minutes, Brian decided to check out the area. The plan when we left Kuujjuaq was that the pilot would land on the lake if the conditions were suitable. If not, he would land in the Arm just beyond it. As Brian explored, I stayed put, because my feet were almost too tender to touch to the ground by this time. I had to limp the last couple of kilometres, and I did not want to aggravate my feet and ankles any more.

The Arm was about a kilometre from the end of the lake, and Brian was soon back to say there was evidence of people having been there recently. There was a partially constructed fish counting fence at the mouth of the brook, and a small inflatable raft and some construction utensils nearby. It seemed certain that the people building the counting fence would return soon. We had seen no one in eighteen days and two hundred kilometres of walking, and were becoming a little hungry for human companionship. We were also curious to find out what had brought them to this remote location.

By noon it had become quite windy outside our little sheltered haven, and we were starting to think the plane might not come for us that day. We decided to lie off in the sun and enjoy it. The water in the lake was quite cold, so we gathered some dead willows and lit a fire to heat some water, changed our clothes, and freshened up a bit. It felt good to be at least semi-clean. Later I washed some clothes in the lake and hung them on the willows to dry in the sun. What a beautiful spot! I was sure there were very few places around that could match this.

After an hour or so my feet felt a little better, and we walked down to the Arm where we found a fibreglass boat tied up and two people on the beach having lunch. We soon introduced ourselves to Milton Shears of St. John's and Eli Merkuratsuk from Nain who were doing some research on arctic char for the Department of Fisheries and Oceans (DFO). Their camp was at Southwest Arm, about twenty minutes away by boat, but they were back and forth to North Arm a couple of times a day. There were several other men back at the camp. It was nice to see other people after so long.

After an enjoyable chat, we walked around the area and did some exploring before returning to our campsite. We found several Inuit burial sites and an old headstone dated 1883. It was weather-worn and difficult to read, but appeared to have been placed there in memory of a Captain A. B. Pidgeon.

The area also contained several large stone caches which had once been used to store char. These were built in open, well-drained locations, and their stone construction would have enabled air to circulate freely while discouraging scavengers. Arctic char were an

112

important food source for the Inuit of Labrador, as well as for their dogs, and they were trapped and netted in rivers all along the coast. While some were eaten fresh, large quantities were dried or salted for later consumption.

As the day wore on with no sign of the plane, we set up our tent and cooked a pot of pea soup over an open fire, supplemented by some carrots and salt riblets which we had packed in our food bag. We made a hearth out of some flat rocks, and I had carried a small grill from an old barbeque in my backpack. It was great! We were both very tired after our early morning rise, so we turned in early. We were hoping there would be no wind the next day so that the plane could get in for us. Although this place was beautiful, we were very restricted in how far we could roam from our campsite because we wanted to be there when the plane came. It limited our exploration of the Arm.

We were up early the next morning and packed everything up except the tent, which we could take down in a couple of minutes. It was a lovely, sunny day with a beautiful, blue sky and only a slight breeze. It seemed like ideal flying weather. After breakfast, we lazed in the sun and walked along the shore of the lake for a little while. By about 10:00 a.m., however, Brian was losing hope that the plane would come that day. The wind usually picked up about mid-day, and he assumed that the pilot would want to be in and out before that time.

Inuit ruins, North Arm.

Ermine at North Arm, Saglek Fiord.

TREKKING THROUGH NORTHERN LABRADOR

The breeze did start to pick up around noon, and we decided to go for a short walk. There had been a massive avalanche down the cliffs on the valley's west side at some time in the past, and we could clearly see where it had swept right across the stream, leaving a large fan of rusty-brown rubble for several hundred metres on the other side. These rocks were home to a family of six or eight ermine (my Dad would call them weasels). They were amazingly quick, and would pop up from among the boulders on all sides to look at us. Brian took several pictures of the curious creatures.

We went back to the tent to take a nap, but jumped at every bee that flew past. They sounded so much like the drone of a small plane in the distance. Just as we were settled in we heard voices, and looked out to see our new friends walking up from the Arm. Milton and Eli told us their work with the Department of Fisheries and Oceans involved carrying out a survey of several of the rivers running into Saglek Fiord, to determine the potential for a commercial char fishery. They had just arrived from their camp at Southwest Arm to finish constructing the counting fence at the mouth of the stream.

We all sat around on rocks by the side of the lake and enjoyed the view and a very pleasant, sunny day. Milton and Eli told us they had a two-way radio at Southwest Arm. They would be making radio contact with Nain in the morning and asked us if we wanted them to convey a message to our families to let them know we were O.K. We did give them a short message to relay back home, indicating we were fine, in the company of some people from Fisheries and Oceans, and waiting for the plane to come and get us. We really appreciated their offer, as we were now overdue and I knew our families would be worried. They also said they would be setting up a small satellite camp at North Arm within the next few days. It was nice to know we weren't stranded here alone.

Later that afternoon, after Milton and Eli left to go back to their camp, we took our fishing rod and walked down to the Arm. A strong, gusty wind was sweeping up through the fiord, and we were glad we had found such a sheltered spot for the tent. It looked quite nasty on the water and I wondered if our friends had gotten back to their camp safely. Although they had told us it was only a few minutes away by speedboat, even a short time on the water in that kind of wind could seem endless. Of course, we didn't know how bad it was outside our immediate area or how much open water they would have to cross.

Arctic char are similar to salmon in that they are born in fresh water, but travel back and forth to salt water at various times throughout their life. They normally migrate upstream in the late summer, and there was a large school of them at the mouth of the stream, where they were becoming acclimatized to the fresh water before making their run up to the lake.

117

Before long we had caught a sizeable char. Since I was always nervous about cleaning fish anywhere near the tent, in case there were bears in the area, Brian filleted it in the stream, afterwards placing a rock in its mouth so the remains would sink to the bottom. Even though we hadn't seen any evidence of bears in this particular valley, we knew they couldn't be too far, as it was ideal country for them. We carried the fish back to our campsite and fried it in pork fat for dinner. It was a substantial and enjoyable meal.

CHAPTER 15

OUR NEIGHBOURS

The next morning was sunny and warm, with only a slight breeze, and I felt confident that the plane would soon arrive. As we packed up, we could hear hammering, and guessed it was our new neighbours setting up camp down by the Arm. They stopped by later that morning and invited us to come down and have some dinner with them, if we were still there at the end of the day.

That would have been a delightful change, but we were hoping the plane would be in to get us before that. Unfortunately, such was not the case. By lunch time we had given up hope of seeing the plane, so I washed some more clothes, hanging them on the bushes to dry.

The runout from the lake seemed to be a favourite crossing place for caribou travelling around the west side of the lake, and we watched as several small companies walked across the stream behind the tent before wandering off along the beach. Later that afternoon we had some light rain showers, so we did some reading in the tent to pass the time.

We walked down to see our friends at about 5:30, seeing several robins along the way. It was unusual to find them this far north. Milton had caught some char which Eli cooked for dinner. Brian had a grand feed, and I was delighted to have some tea with canned milk (a real treat after using powdered milk for over two weeks). Crackers with margarine and jam provided a satisfying dessert.

After dinner Milton and Eli tried to make radio contact with the main camp at Southwest Arm. The signal was poor, and their efforts to relay a list of things they needed brought over by boat the next morning were met with mixed, and at times comical, results. Eventually they managed to get across most things on the list except "salt". After many attempts, the closest the other people could come to salt was "socks". They finally gave up after agreeing to try to make contact in the morning before the boat left Southwest Arm.

We had been curious to learn whether Milton and Eli had experienced any problems during their windy boat ride of the previous evening, and it was now time to hear their story. Apparently, they had encountered some big waves outside North Arm and their outboard motor had come loose from the back of the boat. They managed to get a line around it and get to shore, but had to leave the boat there and walk back to their camp at Southwest Arm. It took them over three hours, as they were wearing heavy fishing waders with steel toes. I'm sure those three hours must have seemed like our all-day treks as they walked over the loose talus slopes around the side of the bay. The people at Southwest Arm had been getting ready to organize a search for them when they finally walked into camp.

The next morning was the start of our fourth day at North Arm, and we were starting to get restless. It seemed incredible that we had not yet been picked up, given the beautiful weather of the past few days, and Brian and I were beginning to wonder if we had simply been forgotten. We should have been back in St. John's by this time, our food was getting low, and a bath and a soft bed were long overdue.

By now we had settled into a routine of getting up for breakfast and packing up some of our gear. As each day passed, we became less and less optimistic, packed up less and less of our gear, and eventually decided not to pack up anything until we actually saw the plane fly over. Milton had a few pocket novels with him, so Brian read a lot during the days. We still hoped the plane would come eventually, and Brian thought that perhaps they would try to get in later in the day, since the wind usually died out in the evening and the long days would still allow us time to get back to Kuujjuaq before dark. After all, the air charter service didn't know we were in the company of other people and, since we were travelling on foot, we certainly wouldn't be carrying very much in terms of extra supplies. We assumed the pilot would fly in to get us at the first possible opportunity.

Eli and Milton were eventually joined by John Melendy, a fisheries consultant working out of St. John's, and by a couple of other Inuit from Nain. We spent each day reading, visited with the fisheries people in the evenings, and did some washing and general sight-seeing. My feet didn't seem to be getting any better, and I found it difficult to walk the kilometre or so down to the other camp, especially when we visited a couple of times during the same day.

By 4:30 it seemed clear that the plane would not be coming again that day, and we walked down to see what the DFO people were doing. They were busy checking the char in the holding pen they had built in the stream, and I offered to cook dinner for them. They gave me full use of their "kitchen", so I cooked some corned beef hash on their propane stove and washed the dishes for them when we were finished.

As I was cleaning up, we saw a herd of caribou

working their way up the side of the Arm, and Eli proceeded to shoot one for some fresh meat over the next week or so. The Inuit hunted for food rather than sport, and would kill the occasional caribou or seal as a way of supplementing their diet while they worked on the char fishery. They had the animal down, cleaned and brought back to camp before I finished the dishes. They were looking forward to a meal of caribou stew the next day.

As the days progressed I found it interesting to watch the Inuit go about their regular routine. They made something called "pipsi" by slicing char fillets into strips which they hung out to dry. They often eat raw meat, and would think nothing of cutting off a piece of uncooked caribou and munching on it. They told us of eating braided seal intestines and raw caribou liver. I didn't find any of this very appetizing. I think I would have to be terribly hungry before I would consider eating seal intestines. John and Milton said they had tried them, and found them to be quite good.

Now that it was August, the days were rapidly becoming shorter, and it was almost dark by the time we got back to our tent. There had been some light showers as the evening came on, and we had waited for a break before we left. I didn't like walking through the willows and alders after dark. The fisheries people had told us about a black bear which had visited their Southwest Arm camp in the middle of the night, putting its two front paws on the roof of a tent and pushing it in on top of the

*Making pipsi from Arctic Char,
North Arm.*

unfortunate resident. Of course, in many cases they slept in the tent with their food supplies and did all of their cooking in there as well. We were very careful not to leave any food in our tent, so I wasn't as worried when we were inside, but I didn't want any bears to jump out of the willows at me after dark.

CHAPTER 16

FAREWELL TO THE TORNGATS

The next morning we made some raisin pancakes for breakfast, still using the original box of pancake mix we had when we started out. I walked out to the brook to get some water, and the lake was absolutely still. The reflection of the mountains in the water was beautiful. There was no wind, and I ran back to the tent to get my camera to capture the scene, but, by the time I got back, there was a slight ripple on the lake and the image was lost.

We got washed up just before the wind picked up and it turned quite cool. Before long, it became overcast, with a strong breeze. There was a smell of smoke in the air, perhaps from some distant forest fire in Quebec, and we speculated that the plane would not come for us again that day.

Later that afternoon we saw Eli tramping through the bushes. He was bent almost double with the weight of the inflatable boat, which he left by the lake in order to do some research the next morning. Just before dinner he returned to bring us some caribou stew. It contained a large part of the tongue of the caribou he had shot the previous evening. Caribou tongue is a great delicacy, and we warmed it up for an early dinner. We were glad to have some solid food to supplement our meagre rations. The sky was very black and, by 4:00 p.m., it had started to rain. I didn't even get out to do the dishes. I just left them overturned outside the tent.

The fine weather returned the next morning, and we had the last little bit of pancake mix and raisins for breakfast. I thought about the box of pancake mix from our food bag which we had burned. We may have been sick of pancakes back then, but now we were wishing we had kept it. We had been substituting jam for pancake syrup for the past few days.

I was just about to add my last half teaspoon of skim milk powder to my tea when it disappeared in a sudden puff of wind. I <u>was not</u> very well pleased! One thing I always look forward to outdoors is a cup of tea. Although I prefer real milk, outdoors I'm not particular as long as its some type of milk product. Whether its powdered or liquid doesn't matter, but when it blows away in the breeze and there is no more, well, that's not my idea of how to start my day off right.

Just as I was about to give up in complete frustration, I saw Eli and John coming through the willows. They brought the paddles for the Zodiac inflatable which had been brought up to the lake the day before, and, most importantly, they had a care package for us - tea bags, dried soup, toilet tissue, crackers, corn flakes, sugar AND A CAN OF MILK! I was so happy. It made my day. Of course, I had to wonder how much longer we would have to go on like this. Our food was getting very scarce by this time, and the little we did have left, such as a couple of onions, a few carrots, and some cheese, was not aging gracefully.

We asked John and Eli if, when they were on the radio to DFO in Nain, they would ask them to send a message to the air charter people in Kuujjuaq to advise that we had been waiting for a week and had run out of food. There seemed to be no reasonable explanation for their failure to pick us up over the past six days. There had been times in North Arm when it was absolutely calm and the weather, generally speaking, had been excellent. Of course, the pilot would need about four hours to fly from Kuujjuaq, pick us up, and get back. I imagined that the need for that long a weather window would lower the odds a bit. In any event, it was just a guessing game to us. We didn't know what was going on. We had advised them in writing of the pickup date and had marked the location on a map before leaving Kuujjuaq, but it was always possible that this had gotten mislaid. Not knowing anything was the worst thing.

It was a great relief to have someone around for company. If we had been there all alone, we would have been getting very worried by this time. Our families probably would have started some type of search. We were very isolated, and few people travel this far north. The chances of someone coming by in boat were slim, and it could be weeks, if at all, before we saw any sign of people. While we had the ELT, we would not have wanted to activate it in the absence of a real emergency.

Since there was no sign of the plane coming for us again that day, I went out to the side of the lake and watched as the DFO people went about their work. They were using the depth sounder to check the bottom characteristics. Eli told me that the lake was like a bowl - sandy around the sides and about thirty metres deep all through the middle. We had all named it "Bursey's Pond" several nights before.

John had told us of a high waterfall which could be clearly seen as they came into North Arm by boat, and Brian decided to climb up the side of the mountain to see if he could get a good view of it. Although we had to cross the stream that flowed from its base every time we visited the DFO camp, we could not see the falls as it was up quite a distance and tucked away in a deep cleft in the mountain. I knew Brian had been hoping to get up there before, but we were restricted as to how much exploring we could do as we couldn't take a chance on missing the plane.

I stayed near the tent in case the plane arrived, and watched Brian as he disappeared behind the first section of the mountain. I did not feel so alone this time when he went out of sight, as our friends were still working away nearby. After about an hour, Brian returned and reported that he had had a hard scrabble to a point about three hundred metres above the Arm that offered a spectacular view of the waterfall.

Our neighbours invited us to join them for the evening meal in their large canvas tent. John had cooked up a bean stew with some sort of toutons. Was it ever good! I did the dishes and Brian went for a couple of buckets of water to earn our keep. That, of course, wasn't expected of us, but we didn't want to impose too much.

Later, we made a campfire on the beach and sat around telling stories. It was a beautiful evening and the Arm was like a mirror. A short distance offshore a brood of harlequin ducks swam slowly by, leaving a perfect "V" in the still water. Discussions have been underway for some time between the federal government and the Government of Newfoundland and Labrador with respect to the establishment of a new national park which would encompass the whole area between Killinek Island and the north side of Saglek Fiord, and we hoped the beauty of this area would be preserved for the enjoyment of future generations. We certainly could have been stranded in a much worse place than this. If we hadn't been so concerned about the non-arrival of the plane, this would have been the perfect place for a relaxing holiday.

We had a discussion about alternate ways for us to get out if the plane didn't show up. In a week or so some of the char in the holding pen would be harvested and a collector boat would be along to pick them up. In an emergency, they would probably take us as far as Nain where we'd be able to get a flight or coastal vessel out. Another week or two seemed too long to wait, but there weren't many options available to us. We didn't want to wear out our welcome with our hosts either, as when our last few scraps of food were gone, we'd have to rely on them a good deal. Granted, we could catch char and maybe even shoot a caribou if we were stuck, but there were other things we would need.

We were expected back at work the next morning, Monday, August 8, but the new day found us still camped at "Bursey's Pond". After breakfast we sat back in the tent for a few minutes as I wrote in my journal. I heard another bee outside the tent - or was it? As I listened, the sound became louder. Brian and I looked at each other and just about tore the door off the tent getting out! We saw the plane over the mountains and jumped and waved, but it flew past us and out of sight. We hurriedly took

down our tent, hoping it was our plane circling around to land. We saw no sign after that, but just as we finished packing up, we saw Milton running through the willows shouting that the plane had landed and was taxiing in to shore. He helped us carry some of our gear down to the Arm.

My feet had not improved at all during the past week, and I told Brian and Milton to go on ahead to let the pilot know we were on our way. I limped through the willows and across the streams, the straps of my pack trailing along behind me and snagging on every stray branch. I moved along as quickly as I could, but I must have looked like a two-legged mule when I finally stumbled down to the beach where the plane was awaiting my arrival. John and Eli greeted me with a movie camera, each looking for a commentary on transportation in northern Labrador.

We said good-bye to some really nice people and headed off. There was a stiff breeze blowing, and our pilot didn't appear very comfortable with it. I hoped my motion sickness pill was going to work!

◄ *A 200 metre waterfall cascades down*
a mountain near North Arm.

CHAPTER 17

GOING HOME

It was quite a rough trip to Kuujjuaq, especially as we climbed over the Torngats, and I was relieved when we finally landed. Reservations had been made for us to fly to Montreal in a couple of hours. When we got out of the plane onto the dock, we got quite a few comments from people who had been there when we left and knew what our plans were. One fellow said, "Well, we didn't expect to see you guys again." One little boy, who had been around the day before we departed, had predicted that we'd be eaten by bears. Of course, for a few minutes during the trip the same thought had crossed my mind as well!

We had left a bag at the float plane base with some clean clothes, shoes and toiletries for when we returned.

GOING HOME

The first thing we did was throw away our sneakers. The sides were gone out of both pairs and even the front of one of Brian's was missing. We then had a quick clean-up and change before being transported to the airport.

During conversations at the dock and on the way to the airport, we were somewhat surprised that the air charter people did not appear to be at all concerned that they had been a week late in picking us up, or that we might have been running out of food. Their attitude did not seem to be very responsible to us. As the old adage goes, "You pay your money and you take your chance".

A few hours later we were on a First Air flight on our way to Montreal. The attendant announced that pepper steak was on the menu and that they would serve wine with the meal. I had to pinch myself to make sure I wasn't still at North Arm with braided seal intestines for dinner! A short while later they made another announcement to the effect that, since the number of passengers boarding in Kuujjuaq had been quite a bit smaller than had been anticipated, they had extra meals if anyone would care for one. Brian just looked at me and grinned. He, of course, took full advantage of the offer.

We landed at Montreal around 6:00 p.m. and, since our flight to St. John's wasn't leaving until the next day, spent the night just outside the city. One of our first priorities was to call our families to let them know we were alright. They had been quite worried when we hadn't made it back for work on time and were quite relieved to hear from us. I had thought about my sister many times during the trip, as she had been due to have a baby while we were gone. I was relieved to find that everything had gone fine and I now had a new nephew named Mark.

We didn't arrive back in St. John's until late the following evening, and went straight to work the next day. It seemed as if we had been around the world and back again in a couple of days.

Everyone was glad to see us back. Even people at work had gotten involved in initiating a search for us when we didn't show up for work on August 8 as expected. We had lots of stories to tell about our adventures, and many of our friends speculated that we probably wouldn't be going back to Labrador any time soon.

That, of course, was not the case. The following summer we returned to Labrador to canoe the Kenamu River, which flows down through the Mealy Mountains and into Lake Melville. We had been on the river for about a week when we reached a ten kilometre long rapid. Several days of heavy rain had swollen the river into a raging torrent, and there were a lot of large standing waves as the current swept over one set of massive boulders after another. Our canoe overturned, spilling us, and was floating downstream though the rapids with all our gear strapped in it. Brian had made it to shore and was shouting, "keep your feet up", as I fought with the river to get to shore ....

But that's another story!